NORTH MARKET COOKBOOK

NORTH MARKET COOKBOOK

Written and Compiled by Robin Davis

Photographs by Ken Heigel

American Foodways Press
2008

NORTH MARKET COOKBOOK
First Edition, First Printing

Text and Recipes © 2008 by Robin Davis
Photographs © 2008 by Ken Heigel
Historic photographs of the North Market on pages 12–15 courtesy
of the Columbus Metropolitan Library, Columbus, Ohio.

ISBN 978-0-89730-250-0

Publisher: Ray Berg
Editor: Ginny Berg
Designer: Jimmy Ball

R.J. Berg Publisher/American Foodways Press
P.O. Box 30225
Indianapolis, IN 46230-0225
1.800.638.3909
www.americanfoodwayspress.com

Printed in China

ACKNOWLEDGMENTS

Like the North Market itself, this book was a group effort. The first contributors, and certainly the most important, were the Market's merchants and farmers. Hearing their stories and memories made me fall in love with the Market on a deeper level. In addition, North Market Executive Director Dave Wible was an enormous help as the gatherer of recipes and the initial go-between for the merchants and me. My thanks also to publisher Ray Berg, who came up with the idea, and Ginny Berg, who was the editor.

Finally, my thanks to my family for their patience at my long hours completing this book. Ben, Molly and Sarah, you never failed to give me encouragement and support. And Ken, your photographs in this book inspired me to write words worthy to accompany them. Thank you for being my partner in this project, and in life.

CONTENTS

Walk into any supermarket and you will find just about everything you need – milk, bread, eggs, meats, greeting cards, flowers, medicines, books. One-stop shopping may fit today's fast pace, but it comes at a price. We no longer have a connection to the food, the producers or the farmers. We don't know where the food came from or what went into making it.

It wasn't always this way.

More than 100 years ago, people in Columbus, Ohio, shopped at their "markets" – not supermarkets, but local gathering places where people bought and sold their wares. In Columbus, four such markets existed, one in each quadrant of the city. People shopped at whichever was closest to where they lived: north, east, west or central. Customers could find everything they needed for their daily lives, and they could also look the milkman in the eye and ask what the cow was fed. They could tell the butcher exactly which cut of meat they wanted. They could ask the farmer if next week they might have strawberries or butter lettuce.

The North Market was the second of these public markets in Columbus. And now it's the only remaining market of its kind in the city.

The North Market opened in 1876, but not at its current location. Then it was located at the city's public cemetery at 29 Spruce Street, which is now the Market's parking lot.

In 1948, the North Market was destroyed by fire, and the city chose not to rebuild. But with determined spirits, the Market's merchants pooled their funds and purchased a Quonset hut, a glorified tent really, to erect on the site so they could continue to sell their products and maintain the sense of community.

But after World War II, Columbus residents – like city dwellers across the country – began to leave downtown for the suburbs, and the early versions of the modern-day supermarket were born, leaving fewer and fewer shoppers for the North Market. By the 1970s, the Market was on a month-to-month lease with the city.

During the 1980s, people across the country started to rediscover their public markets, and revitalization efforts began as a way to reconnect the history of the city with the present day. In Columbus, a group of shoppers and merchants formed the North Market Development Authority, a nonprofit group that worked to preserve and promote the tradition and history of the Market. The Authority saved the North Market from being demolished to make way for a parking lot for the nearby convention center.

The next step was to renovate the Quonset hut. But the Authority realized that such renovations would be too costly and extensive – and the hut was already too small for all of its merchants. Eventually, the city of Columbus purchased a warehouse at nearby 59 Spruce Street for the North Market. The space, a turn-of-the-century farm implements warehouse, turned out to be the ideal building for the new North Market. In 1995, the Market opened with 25 merchants.

Today, the North Market continues to offer items that fill shoppers' daily needs – eggs, cheese, meats and fish – and it also represents the diversity of Columbus with a pizzeria next to an Indian restaurant and a florist backing up to a bubble tea vendor. Some of the 1 million customers who visit the Market each year may come for a single reason – perhaps searching for that perfect fillet of arctic char for a dinner party or a bottle of wine they couldn't find anywhere else in town. But many also come for the experience itself, to buy the freshest produce from local farmers, enjoy a lunch of cassoulet or pho, indulge in a piece of chocolate or a marzipan peach, and take home a bag of caramel corn or a jar of zesty salsa. No other place in Columbus gathers the same mix of people from such varied backgrounds and lifestyles, which makes for wonderful people watching every day.

It's all here at the North Market, which is both a remembrance of days past and a look toward the future.

NORTH MARKET
59 Spruce St
Columbus, OH 43215
614.463.9664

TIMELINE

Central Market, the first public market in Columbus, Ohio, opens on 4th Street between Town and Rich streets.

The Ohio State University opens on farmland several miles north of the capital center.

West Market is established on South Gift Street.

1850	1851	1870	1876	1889	1892

The first Lazarus department store is built at Town and High streets.

North Market, at 29 Spruce Street, becomes the second public market in Columbus. It was located on the city's North Graveyard.

East Market opens on Mount Vernon Avenue.

The Columbus Senators baseball team plays its season at Neil Park. North Market provides the food and drink.

North Market is renovated and redecorated.

There are 125,000 weekly shoppers in Columbus' public markets; 75 percent of the city's population shops at one of the markets weekly.

1900   1910   1914   1916   1917   1918

Nearly 2,000 people are employed in Columbus public markets.

Dorothy Gatterdam begins "on market" selling eggs with her parents at the Central Market.

Heat is installed in all four public markets.

TIMELINE

West Market closes. Business dropped off because the market didn't have a streetcar line passing near it. The building is converted into a recreation center, which continues today.

East Market is destroyed by fire.

Only five of the 50 stalls at North Market are in use.

1926   **1934**   **1947**   **1948**   **1965**   **1966**

Big Bear establishes its first grocery store in Ohio on Lane Avenue, marking the beginning of the boom of the suburbs.

North Market burns down, almost a year to the day after the East Market fire. Later in the year, North Market reopened on the same site in a Quonset hut that was purchased by the Market's merchants.

Central Market is demolished as part of an urban renewal project. It is replaced by a Greyhound bus station that is still there today. Fifteen Central Market merchants, including Dorothy Gatterdam, move to the North Market.

The North Market
Historic District is listed
on the National Register
of Historic Places.

The North Market
Development Authority
is formed. The city of
Columbus enters into a
five-year lease with the
Authority to plan the
Market's future.

North Market formally
opens in a renovated
warehouse at 59 Spruce
Street, adjacent to the
site of the original
market.

1980 **1982** **1988** **1993** **1995** **TODAY**

The seasonal farmers'
market is reintroduced
at the North Market.

The Columbus
Convention Center
opens.

North Market is home to
more than 30 merchants
as well as a host of
farmers at the Saturday
farmers' market. It is also
the location for popular
festivals, including the
Harvest Festival and the
Columbus Microbrew
Festival.

Over the years, the merchants at the North Market have come and gone. Only one original vendor remains "on market": Gatterdam Eggs. But the spirit of the place has not wavered.

The North Market offers a sense of community that is palpable to anyone who walks through the doors. Ask any of the merchants why they chose the North Market as a space for their business and they will tell you it's because of the familylike feeling. Each merchant brings his or her own passion to their business, making the North Market, to paraphrase Aristotle, greater than the sum of its merchants.

Where else can you get cheddar-dusted popcorn and an environmentally friendly household cleaner in the same building? And where else will the baker remember that you love the focaccia squares or the butcher know that you'll surely be in for steaks on Friday for your weekly grill-out?

And where else can you go to sit in the shade at a table on the covered patio and enjoy music while having lunch – or at a table on the second floor overlooking the bustling Market when the weather turns cool?

The genuine community spirit of the North Market merchants instantly spills over to the Market's shoppers.

THE ARCHIVE VINTAGE ARTS AND CUSTOM FRAMING

BARRY'S NEW YORK STYLE DELI

Sarah Karlsberger has been a merchant at the North Market just since 2005, but she's been a customer and lover of the Market since she was a child.

The Archive, she says, is a combination of her two loves: picture framing and antiques. Both help people preserve memories and traditions. Opening a shop at the North Market did the same for Karlsberger.

Her shop specializes in custom framing, but customers can also purchase antique artwork and photographs, maps, china and one-of-a-kind vintage jewelry.

You don't have to go to New York for a true deli sandwich. Barry Rosenthal, with his son Larry, creates a bite of the Big Apple in the North Market every day.

Customers agree: Barry's corned beef – cooked on site – is the best in the city. No wonder; Bronx-born and Long Island–raised, Barry knows good deli.

Barry's has been an institution at the Market since 1996, when Barry opened the deli on his birthday. Larry adds his own twist to the family business with his homemade cheesecake – New York style, of course.

BEST OF THE WURST

This gourmet hot dog stand has been part of the North Market since the Quonset hut era. It's owned by Nida Sujirapinyokul and Chris Perry, who started "on market" with Nida's Sushi across the aisle.

As one might expect, Best of the Wurst specializes in sausages, plus top-notch all-beef hot dogs and sandwiches. The shop also sells a variety of sausages, imported meats and condiments – especially mustards – for customers to take home.

BETTER EARTH AND
BETTER EARTH BEYOND BEADS

Originally, the North Market was where merchants sold food. But in its current iteration, the Market has room for restaurants and other products such as the environmentally conscious aromatherapy products, cleaning solutions and gift items at Better Earth and the gorgeous jewelry at Beyond Beads. Both stalls are under the direction of Dareen Wearstler.

Wearstler opened Better Earth in the Quonset hut in 1991, then moved into the shop's current space. In 2005, she paired her talents with that of artist Theresa Colson to open a shop that sells fabulous hand-crafted necklaces, earrings and more. Wearstler also offers beads and classes on jewelry making.

BLUESCREEK FARM MEATS

Bluescreek is more than a butcher shop. Owners Cheryl and David Smith raise the cattle, lambs, pigs and goats that provide the meats they sell at the Market. All of their animals are raised without growth hormones or antibiotics.

The Smiths came to the North Market in 1993 when the Market's previous butcher shop closed. Unlike the prepackaged meats found in supermarkets, the meat at Bluescreek is freshly butchered by David. The whirring sound of the ban saw is a part of the daily din of the Market as meats are cut to stock the case or for special orders.

Bluescreek also specializes in oven-ready meatloaf. Cheryl says they sell about 40 pounds each week. When not making the meatloaf, she spends much of her time giving shoppers recipes and suggesting cooking techniques for their meats – customer service that is a Bluescreek hallmark.

BUBBLES: THE TEA AND JUICE COMPANY

CAJOHN'S FLAVOR AND FIRE

What's a guy with two degrees from Ohio State doing with a smoothie shop? Working for himself and loving it, says Eric Ling, owner of Bubbles.

Bubbles' customers love the smoothies, from a citrus serenade of orange juice and strawberries to a creamy cookies 'n' cream with Oreos and chocolate milk. In addition to smoothies, Ling offers milk bubble teas – assorted teas mixed with milk and poured over tapioca pearls or cubes of coconut jelly – and fresh juices, including shots of wheatgrass juice.

A bubble tea purveyor fits in perfectly with the Market's eclectic mix of merchants and the adventurous clientele.

You like it hot? Then you'll love CaJohn's, one of the newest additions to the North Market.

Owner and chili pepper expert John Hard decided he needed a retail outlet in addition to his specialty food product manufacturing facility in Columbus. The North Market, which plays host to a chili pepper festival in the spring, seemed like the perfect venue.

Hard sells a variety of salsas, hot sauces and seasonings, all made in small batches and all of which express his passion: hot and spicy foods with flavor, not just heat. His products are loved across the country; in fact, he's won more than 100 first-place awards for spicy foods.

CHINA MARKET

CURDS AND WHEY

The lunchtime line that snakes down the corridor for one of the dozens of China Market's made-to-order Asian dishes is proof of the popularity of this North Market staple. Many customers – as well as the press – say China Market serves the best pad thai in Columbus. Shoppers can also buy a variety of hard-to-find Asian products, from hot sauces and noodles to spices and rice.

The North Market has always included some kind of cheese shop. Since 1988, Curds and Whey has been under the ownership of Mike Kast, who has also owned, at different points in the Market's history, Grapes of Mirth and Best of the Wurst.

Today, Kast focuses on his worldwide selection of cheese. He promotes local products such as Oakvale Farm's raw milk Farmstead Gouda (see page 40) and Lake Erie Creamery chèvre, and he is also knowledgeable about cheese from other parts of the globe, including Roquefort from France, manchego from Spain and Britain's wide range of cheddars. Columbus restaurateurs rely on Kast to help create cheese plates – an increasingly popular selection at upscale eateries – while Market shoppers know he's the go-to guy for any questions about cheese.

FIRDOUS EXPRESS

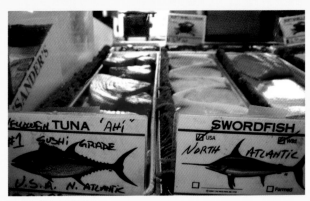

THE FISH GUYS

Anyone who thinks Midwesterners aren't cosmopolitan might be surprised to see Firdous Express, one of the many eateries at the Market. They might be even more surprised to know that this restaurant specializing in Mediterranean fare has been part of the Market since it moved into its permanent space in 1995. The long line of customers at the stall each day tells the story of this restaurant's success.

Abdul Aburmaieleh took over the reins from longtime owner Nasir Latif in 2006 and continues to make the crunchy falafel, stuffed grape leaves, shawarma and flaky-sweet baklava, to name just a few of the customer favorites.

While there isn't an ocean anywhere near Columbus, The Fish Guys provide seafood lovers with all the fish and shellfish they need. Bob Reany opened the stall in 1995, then sold the business to Doug Denny in 2006.

Like Reany, Denny sells a large selection of the freshest seafood such as live lobsters, scallops, various sizes of shrimp, and wild salmon when it's in season. Customers can also enjoy a number of specialties at lunch, including crab cakes, shrimp or lobster salad, and fish and chips.

FLAVORS OF INDIA

GATTERDAM EGGS

More than just a restaurant serving delectable Indian specialties, Flavors of India doubles as a shop where customers can buy hard-to-find Indian ingredients including whole cardamom pods, curry leaves, asafetida, tamarind paste and, of course, curry powders. But most of the customers come for the food: palak paneer with creamy Indian cheese, succulent lamb curry, and chana masala packed with chickpeas.

Like many of the other merchants, Flavors of India has been part of the North Market since the Quonset hut days. Raj Brar and his wife, Billan, took over the restaurant in 1991.

If there is one business that captures the essence of the North Market history, it's Gatterdam Eggs. The oldest business at the Market, Gatterdam has been part of the scenery since 1916 when it was located at the now-closed Central Market. The original owner, Dorothy Gatterdam, transplanted the business to the North Market in 1966 when the Central Market was demolished to make way for the Greyhound bus station.

Today, Gatterdam sells eggs by the honor system: Customers put money in the lockbox and take their eggs. Sounds quaint, but it works. Bill Thompson, who is married to Gatterdam's niece, manages the stall and says he sells between 400 dozen and 500 dozen eggs a week. That's not chicken scratch.

GRAPES OF MIRTH

HEIL FAMILY DELI

Maybe the original North Market didn't sell wine. And maybe during Prohibition, the only liquor that customers could get was moonshine, sold on the sly by an industrious merchant or two. But today, a wine merchant is a must-have for an urban market catering to a wide range of tastes.

Grapes of Mirth has been part of the Market since 1990, when it was originally named North Market Wines. In 2003, Dave Bihn, a long-time employee at the Market with various merchants, bought the shop. He sells wines from around the world, including a selection of ever-expanding made-in-Ohio wines, which are celebrated at the Food and Ohio Wine Festival, one of many festivities held at the Market throughout the year. Bihn specializes in small-producer wines, selections you're not likely to find at a supermarket.

Want potato salad in Columbus? Go to Heil's. The recipe used here is the same one they've been making since 1954, when then-owner Wayne Heil was the biggest deli salad manufacturer between New York and Chicago.

Of course, that's not the only thing customers enjoy here. Shoppers at Heil's, now owned by Alex Kushkin, can have made-to-order sandwiches or grab one of the premade egg salad, ham and cheese, or turkey creations. Round out the meal with some homemade soup, then pick up a pound or two of your favorite deli meat to make sandwiches at home. Just be sure to get a side order of the delicious potato salad.

JENI'S FRESH ICE CREAMS

signature salty caramel – on the menu year-round while rotating in seasonal favorites, including crème de violet and strawberry buttermilk, based as much as possible on what's grown and produced in central Ohio.

JOSÉ MADRID SALSA

Jeni Britton has been one of the great success stories of the North Market – but her first venture "on market," another ice cream place called Scream, didn't fare as well. It closed in 1999.

The current shop, which opened in 2002, is so successful she's been featured on the Food Network's "Roker on the Road" as well as being named one of *Food & Wine* magazine's top young talents in 2006. Her ice creams are also featured at many Columbus restaurants.

One taste of her unique flavor creations tells the whole story: black coffee that gives creamy just-roasted java a decadent stage from which to sing, tart lemon yogurt swirled with blueberries, or meltingly sweet Savannah buttermint. Britton keeps some staples – such as her

The smoky aroma of roasting chili peppers and spices often fills the air early in the morning at the North Market – and the culprit is José Madrid Salsa, where owner Mike Zakany has been making salsas for years.

Customers can sample Zakany's salsas and his homemade tortilla chips each day. Try various tomato-based concoctions, sweet-and-spicy strawberry or raspberry salsas, or specialty items such as roasted garlic and olive salsa.

LAC VIET MARKET

MARKET BLOOMS

For those who love the fresh flavors of Vietnamese cuisine, Lac Viet is the place to go. Thang Nguyen whips up banh mi (Vietnamese sandwiches), pho (beef noodle soup) and, of course, coffee Viet Nam style: mixed with sweetened condensed milk and poured over ice. Main courses are served in oversized bowls, evidence of the value of this eatery. For just a few bucks, customers can eat like kings.

A public market without a flower stand wouldn't be worth its weight in seed. Market Blooms fills that role at the North Market beautifully.

In the center of the Market, near the main entrance, Market Blooms adds color and fragrance with its array of cut flowers, which can range from delicate daffodils in the spring to sunny sunflowers in the late summer and an assortment of other blooms the rest of the year.

Owner Marty McGreevy acquired the shop from the previous owner in 1990 and has been going strong ever since. Her arrangements, and those of her employees, are some of the most sought-out in the

city – and for good reason. Her penchant for color and use of unusual ingredients, including fruits and vegetables, make the creations particularly artistic.

MOZART'S BAKERY

For fine European pastries in Columbus, Mozart's is the place to go. The North Market location is the second of three in the city for the Austrian couple who own the bakery.

Doris Saha creates the German- and Austrian-inspired baked goods – everything from marzipan confections

that look like peaches to decadent layered chocolate tortes and five kinds of petits fours. In addition, the store offers cookies, biscotti and cannoli.

At the Market, shoppers can buy a slice of cake for dessert after lunch or pick up cookies or pastries to take to the office or enjoy on the outdoor patio. For special occasions, Saha and her staff come up with creations ranging from birthday cakes to multi-tiered wedding cake masterpieces.

NIDA'S SUSHI

NORTH MARKET COOKWARE

Sushi has become a mainstay in American dining, and the North Market holds its own with Nida's Sushi.

Owners Nida Sujirapinyokul and Chris Perry turn out ultra-fresh sushi – everything from California rolls to tuna or yellowtail nigiri. The stall also specializes in a variety of Thai dishes including luscious tom ka gai (chicken and coconut milk soup). The luckiest customers can grab one of the handful of stools at the tiny bar; the rest have to take their orders to go.

For those who want to make sushi at home, Nida's has all you need, from the perfect rice and vinegar to sushi-grade fish and seaweed.

Not only can shoppers get the freshest foods at the North Market, they can also get the pots and pans in which to cook them.

Kay Davenport opened North Market Cookware in 1999. She sells enamel-covered cast-iron pots from Le Creuset, stainless steel cookware from All-Clad and bakeware from Doughmakers, as well as knives and a host of other gadgets essential for the well-stocked kitchen.

NORTH MARKET POULTRY AND GAME

NORTH MARKET PRODUCE

While most people have become accustomed to buying chicken neatly wrapped in cellophane packaging at the supermarket, North Market Poultry and Game gives customers a completely different experience. Shoppers can purchase a single chicken breast, half chicken, whole chicken or even backs, necks and feet for chicken stock or soup. In addition, owner Annmarie Wong can tell customers how the birds were raised.

But that's not all. North Market Poultry and Game, which made the move to its permanent location under Wong's direction, also sells locally raised turkeys, venison, ostrich, rabbits and more. In addition, customers can feast on the stall's prepared food, from chicken and dumplings or chicken tortilla wraps to cassoulet in winter.

In the beginning, produce was one of the primary components of the North Market, with multiple farmers selling their fruits and vegetables. Now, only one stall sells produce, except on Saturdays during the summer when the farmers' market is in session.

Steve Beard purchased North Market Produce from the previous owners who had worked at the Market for years. He brings in the freshest fruits and vegetables year-round, stocking both the standards – including root vegetables and Brussels sprouts – as well as the unusual, for which, he says, North Market shoppers have an affinity. At North Market Produce, customers will find lychees, rambutan, cherimoya and kumquats alongside strawberries, tomatoes and apples.

OMEGA ARTISAN BAKING

PAM'S MARKET POPCORN

Amy Lozier, owner-baker of Omega, is a third-generation North Market shopper. She remembers coming to the Market with her grandfather and then with her mother. Now, when Lozier's grown daughter visits the Market, she stops by her mother's stall for croissants, scones and handmade breads including focaccia and crispy baguettes.

Lozier opened Omega in August 2003 after working as a pastry chef at various Columbus restaurants. The corner spot seems to have always been a bakery, but it's Omega with staying power, evidenced by the lines that wait daily to scoop up cinnamon rolls, pepperoni rolls or ham-and-cheese-stuffed croissants fresh out of the oven.

Pam Tylka grew up eating Garrett's popcorn in Chicago, so when it came time for her to start her own business, popcorn seemed like a natural. She opened Pam's Market Popcorn in October 2005, making cheddar, caramel, sweet-and-salty and a variety of seasonal favorites, and it's been a big hit among North Market shoppers – and beyond.

Tylka started a program using customer donations to pay for shipping her popcorn to troops overseas. Her stall is adorned with grateful letters from the soldiers, who love the "comfort food" treat from the States.

PASTARIA AND
PASTARIA SECONDA

The pasta at Pastaria and its sister stall across the aisle is so popular, some Italian restaurants in Columbus buy it to serve in their dining rooms. For North Market customers, the pasta can be enjoyed as a meal right there, topped with sauce and served with any number of salads, then finished with a slab of tiramisù. Alternately, shoppers can take the freshly made pasta home and cook it for a family meal or dinner party.

Pastaria specializes in filled pastas: zebra-striped pasta enclosing lobster, pink pasta filled with creamy mascarpone, and pink-and-white-striped pasta enclosing a Brie and sun-dried tomato filling. Sauces run the gamut from wildly spiced arrabbiata to mild and cheesy Alfredo. For special occasions, Pastaria makes a mean lasagna, either filled with three cheeses or with tiny meatballs and hard-boiled eggs (unusual but delicious).

The stall started at the Quonset hut and was "inherited" by Don Ziliak in 1993. He moved the stall to its current location, then purchased Sarefino's (see page 34). Finally, he opened Pastaria Seconda in 1998, making him the trifecta owner at the North Market.

PURE IMAGINATION CHOCOLATIER

SAREFINO'S PIZZERIA AND ITALIAN DELI

Daniel Cooper's chocolate shop represents the high-end aspect of the North Market. His confections are as beautiful as art: tiny chocolate truffles containing meltingly decadent ganache in an array of flavors. His selection changes all the time but among the favorites are Midnight Extra Dark, perhaps the deepest, darkest chocolate truffle available anywhere; Japanese Jumping Bean, chocolate topped with a neon green wasabi drop; and Pearls of Imagination, a truffle topped with minuscule bits of chocolate-coated puffed rice.

The demand for Cooper's chocolate reaches across the United States. He's even prepared confections for the Hollywood elite including Ben Affleck, Bruce Willis and Brad Pitt.

Grab a slice or two at this authentic New York–style pizzeria or buy a whole pie. This stall specializes in thin-crust pizzas with the traditional toppings: cheese, meats or veggies. Customers can also order cheese-stuffed calzones, meat-studded strombolis or specialty Italian deli meats such as prosciutto and mortadella by the pound.

THE SOURCE BY WASSERSTROM

A TOUCH OF EARTH

Since 2002, Rodney Wasserstrom, owner of Wasserstrom's Restaurant Supply in Columbus, has had an outlet at the North Market. Here he sells discontinued or overstocked plates, glasses and other table-setting paraphernalia at discount prices. Check back often to find an ever-changing array of diner-style coffee mugs, tiny salt and pepper shakers, platters, plates and sundae glasses.

No public market would be complete without a coffee stand. But while customers can buy a cup of joe or a foamy cappuccino at A Touch of Earth, they can also pick up any number of hard-to-find spices, whole bean coffee, dried fruits, beans, grains and baking chocolates.

The farmers at the North Market tell the tale of all farmers throughout the state. You'll know when the weather has been harsh, as when a late frost killed most of the tree fruit blossoms leaving many of the orchard farmers with nothing to sell. Or when the heat and rain have been perfect and sweet corn and tomatoes are in generous supply.

It's the farmers who also let customers know about emerging trends. They bring the same squash blossoms or microgreens to the Market that they sell to chefs, and they tell shoppers about new varieties of potatoes or heirloom tomatoes they've just harvested.

They're also happy to talk about how to enjoy what they've grown, from juicy ripe peaches that can be eaten right out of hand to fresh-shelled peas that should be blanched today to maintain their sweetness even if you don't plan to eat them until tomorrow.

ANDERSON ORCHARD

Stop by the North Market farmers' market to look for asparagus in the spring and apples, cider and pumpkins in the fall from this Pickerington farm. And don't miss the cut flowers all summer long. Some shoppers call farm owner Steve Anderson "the sunflower guy," and for good reason – his sunflower bunches are about the same size as a small child!

BRIDGMAN FARM

Farm owner Mary Bridgman quit the day job she held for 30 years – as a reporter at the *Columbus Dispatch* – to work full-time at her true passion: her 67-acre farm in Washington Court House. Shoppers can look for a variety of vegetables including cabbage, peppers and onions, but her heirloom tomatoes aren't to be missed. Don't be put off by their less-than-perfect appearance. The best heirloom varieties are grown for taste, not for beauty.

COMBS FRESH HERBS

Clelia Combs started selling herbs at the North Market farmers' market in 1988, before anyone else sold fresh herbs. Now many farmers offer them, so Combs has expanded her selections to include vegetables and cut flowers – something about which she's particularly knowledgeable: She used to sell flowers with her six brothers and three sisters at farmers' markets in Italy, her homeland.

EHMANN AND SONS GREENHOUSES

While most of the farmers at the North Market farmers' market offer fruits and vegetables and a few sell cut flowers, Gene Ehmann loads his truck full of potted plants and hanging baskets of perennials and annuals. This is where many Market shoppers get colorful flowers and plants for their yards in the summer.

ELIZABETH TELLING FARMS

This farm, located about 120 miles north of Columbus in Barnesville, brings something more to the North Market than just farm-fresh lettuce, broccoli, potatoes and peas. Owner Sandy Sterrett started a community-supported agriculture project to which customers can subscribe. Then, during the summer, they  each receive a weekly box of locally grown herbs and produce, including some lesser known plants such as stinging nettles, and fresh eggs.

GYPSY BEES

 Kevin Roberts gives the farmers' market at the North Market the feeling of a simpler time. He sells honey, beeswax, candles, jams and an assortment of Amish crafts, including baskets. Roberts often sets up shop in the North Market's plaza or at a vacant stall indoors during the colder months, so his products are available year-round.

H-W ORGANIC FARMS

The North Market isn't the only place where Jim and Sharon Patterson sell produce from their 44-acre farm in Sullivan, but they love the friendly people here. And Jim says the folks at the North Market aren't shy about telling him how much they love his sweet corn. H-W is also known for its cucumbers, green beans and tomatoes – which are so good, Whole Foods even buys them.

JUST THIS FARM

Owner Kevin Eigel quit a lucrative job in the energy business to farm his few acres in Hilliard. All of the produce at Just This Farm is certified organic, from the blackberries and edamame to asparagus and spinach. But what he's known for is garlic – Eigel  grows hard-neck garlic, which he says is more mellow and flavorful than the heads available at supermarkets. Eigel has also started a seed business so others who want to grow his crops can purchase the seeds directly from him.

OAKVALE FARM

When Dale King decided to sell his artisan cheese at a farmers' market, he knew the North Market was the place for him. It was a quick drive from his farm in London, and he and his wife, Jean, often came to the Saturday market to shop. But more importantly, the North Market had been their first customer.

When Mike Kast of Curds and Whey discovered how good Oakvale's raw milk Farmstead Gouda is, he began to stock the cheese at his shop. Soon others took notice too. The cheese, available in regular, aged, caraway, jalapeño and habanero, is sold at Murray's Cheese Shop in New York – considered the Tiffany of cheese shops – and is now available through the Williams-Sonoma catalog.

The Kings are still at the farmers' market each Saturday, offering shoppers tastes of the product that was born out of necessity for them. When their farm with 80 Holsteins and a handful of Brown Swiss didn't produce enough milk to make a profit, the Kings turned to cheese making – a great decision for anyone who's tasted their cheese.

THE ORCHARD OF BILL AND VICKY THOMAS

Much of a farmer's success is dependent on the weather; just ask Bill and Vicky Thomas, who farm 10 acres near Zanesville. One year, an Easter frost virtually wiped out all of their peaches, grapes and plums. But for years, their stall at the North Market has been where shoppers stopped for a sweet taste of Ohio-grown grapes and fresh-pressed apple cider. They plan to be back "on market" – as long as the weather cooperates.

PERSINGER FARMS

Look for Cathy Persinger and her produce from Jamestown at the tower end of the North Market farmers' market. She's there every Saturday selling tomatoes, green beans, eggplant, cabbage and onions.

QUIVERFULL FAMILY FARM

Jim Barr's dream is to retire from his full-time job as a high school counselor to concentrate on his first love: farming. Barr's passion is apparent in the products he sells at the North Market farmers' market: hand-shucked popcorn (including a special scarlet-and-gray mix for Ohio State fans), stone-ground wheat flour and homemade granola.

RHOADS FARM

When it's fruit shoppers want, they head to the

Rhoads Farm stand, which sells succulent strawberries in the spring, tiny raspberries and blackberries in early summer, and juicy peaches, cantaloupes and watermelons the rest of the season. But shoppers can also buy vegetables from this Circleville farm stand – from sweet corn to green beans.

SOMERSET HERBS

Margaret Wince started selling herbs and perennials at the North Market farmers' market in 2000. Now she sells produce too, including 35 kinds of heirloom tomatoes in every color from yellow to pink to brown. Wince says customers always ask her which tomatoes are great for BLTs – to which she replies, "All of them."

SUMMER THYME FARM

Those looking for something special in the way of annuals for the garden know to check out Summer

Thyme Farm at the North Market farmers' market. Delayne Williams and Lynn Miller specialize in hard-to-find annuals from their greenhouses in Marysville. But those seeking something more traditional such as herbs and tomato plants won't be disappointed either; the duo sells plenty. Not into gardening at all? Then stop by and purchase a bag of fresh-picked basil at its peak.

SWEETWATER PONDEROSA

Amy Forrest farms 800 acres in Mechanicsburg, but she considers Kevin Eigel, who farms just a few acres at Just This Farm in Hilliard, something of a mentor. In fact, she shares a stand with him at the North Market farmers' market. Forrest raises a number of specialty crops such as purple plum radishes, but she also specializes in chickens – not mass-produced chickens but ones that are kept outdoors in cages where they can move about and feed naturally. The difference is apparent in the color of the fat (yellow, not white) and the flavor of the meat.

TOAD HILL FARM

Tim Patrick chose the North Market for selling his produce because it was the biggest farmers' market in the area. Fifteen years later, he's still at the Market because he likes the customers. And the customers like him too, especially his lettuces.

TOBY RUN GROWERS

Want mushrooms other than plain-Jane white buttons? During the summer, Jim Rockwell's booth at the North Market farmers' market is where to go. He offers mainly shiitake and oyster mushrooms, including some in lovely pink and yellow hues. Even though the color fades when the mushrooms cook, these fungi are rich in the woodsy flavor of wild mushrooms.

WAYWARD SEED FARM

WISHWELL FARM PRODUCE

Those looking for distinctive, even unusual, produce should stop by this stand each Saturday. Adam Welly and Todd Shriver specialize in produce that restaurant chefs desire, from delicate squash blossoms, shelled peas, a variety of lettuces and diminutive microgreens. They're also experimenting with 50 varieties of heirloom tomatoes.

Customers can't wish for more than they get from Wishwell Farm: asparagus and strawberries in the spring; raspberries, sweet corn and tomatoes in the summer; and winter squash in the fall.

The diverse selection of food items available for purchase at the North Market and its Saturday farmers' market is wonderful! And who better to know how to put these ingredients to use than those who sell them?

The North Market's merchants and farmers shared recipes they love – time-honored traditions they've been serving to their families for years. Some recipes such as Jeni's Amazing Caramel Sauce are served at the stalls. Others, including the Thai Peanut and Popcorn Crusted Chicken from Pam's Popcorn, use the ingredients available for sale. Still others, from merchants who don't sell food, such as Sarah Karlsberger of The Archive, give a glimpse into the kitchens of Midwestern cooks.

MAKES ABOUT 3 CUPS

This eggplant purée from Firdous Express can be served with warmed pita bread or toasted pita chips. It's also great layered with tomatoes and lettuce on a baguette for a vegetarian sandwich.

3 eggplants
½ cup tahini (see Note)
4 garlic cloves
4 tablespoons olive oil
1 teaspoon lemon salt

Preheat oven to 400 degrees.

Poke the eggplants in several places with a fork. Place on a baking sheet. Roast in oven until very soft.

When cool enough to handle, peel eggplant and place in food processor. Add tahini, garlic, olive oil and lemon salt. Process to desired consistency.

Note: Tahini is a sesame seed paste available at Middle Eastern markets and in the international section of some supermarkets.

Bacalhau (Cod Fish Casserole)

MAKES 6 TO 8 SERVINGS

"This is my father's recipe — with my adaptations — that I have served on many Christmas Eves," says Dareen Wearstler of Better Earth. Serve this dish on crackers or toasted baguette slices.

1	pound salt cod chips or pieces
5	large potatoes
	Olive oil
4	garlic cloves, crushed
3	bell peppers (green, orange and yellow or all one color), seeded, sliced
2	large onions, sliced
	Nonstick cooking spray
3	hard-boiled eggs, sliced
	Ground black pepper
	Sliced black olives (preferably Greek)
2	tablespoons finely chopped fresh parsley

Soak fish in water for 8 to 10 hours or overnight, changing the water several times.

Place fish in a pan of clean water. Boil 15 minutes. Drain. Flake fish into bite-size pieces.

Boil potatoes until tender. Drain. When cool enough to handle, peel and slice.

Heat a large skillet with 1 or 2 tablespoons olive oil over medium-high heat. Add garlic, peppers and onions. Cook until tender.

Preheat oven to 350 degrees. Mist a 3-quart baking dish with cooking spray.

Layer the potatoes, fish, eggs and onion mixture in prepared pan. Season with pepper. Sprinkle with olives and parsley. (Dish can be prepared to this point 1 day ahead. Cover and refrigerate. Bring to room temperature before baking.)

Drizzle olive oil over the entire casserole. Cover and bake 30 minutes.

MAKES ABOUT 3 CUPS

This recipe from Firdous Express is a twist on the traditional hummus made with chickpeas. Serve this with pita triangles or as a dip for vegetables.

2   cans (16 ounces each) black beans, drained
1   cup tahini (see Note)
3 to 5 garlic cloves
2   teaspoons ground cumin
2   teaspoons dried oregano
1   teaspoon salt

Blend all ingredients in a food processor until smooth.

Note: Tahini is a sesame seed paste available at Middle Eastern markets and in the international section of some supermarkets.

Cannellini Bean Purée

MAKES 8 TO 10 SERVINGS

Serve this recipe from Pastaria with toasted baguette slices, crackers or as a dip for vegetables.

- 2 pounds dried cannellini beans
- 2 to 4 heads garlic
  Olive oil
- 2 cups grated Romano cheese
- 2 tablespoons lemon juice
  Salt

Place beans in a large pot. Cover with water by 3 inches. Let stand for 8 to 10 hours or overnight. Drain.

Return beans to pot. Add enough water to cover by 3 inches. Bring to a boil. Reduce heat and simmer until beans are tender, about 1 hour.

Meanwhile, preheat oven to 400 degrees.

Cut the top ¼ inch from each head of garlic and discard. Place garlic heads in a small baking dish. Drizzle with olive oil. Cover with foil and roast until garlic is tender, about 45 minutes. When cool enough to handle, squeeze garlic out of papery skins and into food processor.

Drain cooked beans. Add to food processor along with cheese and lemon juice. Purée until smooth. With processor running, gradually add enough olive oil to make desired consistency. Season to taste with salt.

MAKES 6 TO 8 SERVINGS

This is a favorite recipe of John Hard of CaJohn's Flavor and Fire.

1   can whole pickled jalapeño peppers, drained, rinsed
¾   pound sharp aged cheese (such as Parmesan), grated
⅔   cup cream cheese
¼   cup half-and-half
2   tablespoons chipotle chili powder (such as CaJohn's Chipotle Select),
     plus additional for garnish

Cut off stem end of peppers. Slice peppers in half lengthwise and remove seeds.

Mix aged cheese, cream cheese, half-and-half and 2 tablespoons chipotle chili powder. Stuff jalapeños with cheese mixture. Arrange on platter. Sprinkle with additional chipotle chili powder.

Variation: Slice fresh jalapeños and remove seeds and veins. Stuff with cheese mixture. Place on broiler rack in oven. Cover and broil until cheese is bubbly. Transfer to a platter. Sprinkle with chipotle chili powder.

Four Pepper Shrimp and Scallop Ceviche

MAKES 6 TO 8 SERVINGS

The Fish Guys love this use of fresh shrimp and scallops where the acid in the citrus juice "cooks" the shellfish.

24 sea scallops, foot removed, halved
24 large shrimp, peeled, diced into chunks
 2 lemons, juiced
 2 limes, juiced
 1 bunch fresh cilantro, stems removed
 1 jalapeño pepper, finely diced
 1 orange bell pepper, seeded, thinly sliced
 1 red bell pepper, seeded, thinly sliced
 1 yellow bell pepper, seeded, thinly sliced
½ cup finely diced red onion
¼ cup finely diced garlic
 1 tablespoon olive oil
   Salt and pepper
 8 ounces mung bean sprouts

Combine all ingredients except half of the cilantro and the bean sprouts. Season to taste with salt and pepper. Cover and refrigerate at least 4 hours.

Serve over bean sprouts and garnish with reserved cilantro.

MAKES ABOUT 1 CUP

This recipe from Mike Kast of Curds and Whey is a variation on the usual Greek yogurt dish. Serve it with toasted pita triangles.

½   medium-size cucumber, peeled, seeded, chopped or shredded
½   teaspoon salt plus additional to taste
5½ ounces soft fresh goat cheese (such as Montrachet)
1   garlic clove, minced
1   tablespoon chopped fresh herbs such as parsley, oregano, marjoram or a mix
1   tablespoon fresh lemon juice
1   tablespoon olive oil
    Ground black pepper

Mix cucumber and ½ teaspoon salt. Let stand 20 minutes. Drain, squeezing out as much liquid as possible.

Place goat cheese in a small bowl. Add cucumber and all remaining ingredients. Mix well.

Can be served immediately but flavor will improve if mixture is refrigerated for 1 hour.

Herb Cheese Balls

MAKES ABOUT 8 SMALL BALLS

Here's a simply great recipe from Summer Thyme Farm. You can use the cheese balls on their own as a spread, drop them onto hot cooked vegetables or serve them with salad.

8   **ounces cream cheese, room temperature**
1   **cup finely chopped mixed fresh herbs: chives, parsley, rosemary, sage, thyme**

Shape cream cheese into plum-size balls. Roll in herbs.

MAKES 8 ROLLS

This recipe from Thang Nguyen at Lac Viet is the perfect summer appetizer. Unlike Chinese egg rolls, these aren't fried; instead, they are light and fresh, filled with shrimp and vegetables.

2   ounces dried rice noodles (rice vermicelli, see Note)
8   round rice paper wrappers (8¼-inch diameter, see Note)
12 medium shrimp, cooked, peeled, sliced in half lengthwise
8   small sprigs fresh cilantro, mint or Thai basil
8   small Boston lettuce leaves
   Vietnamese Dipping Sauce (recipe follows)
   Peanut Sauce (recipe follows)

Cook rice noodles according to package directions. Drain. Set aside.

Fill a medium bowl with hot water. Working with 3 wrappers at a time, dip each into hot water for about 5 seconds to soften. Lay wrappers individually on a flat surface. Lay 3 shrimp halves, cut side up, horizontally just above the center of each wrapper. Layer a scant ¼ cup noodles over the shrimp, followed by a sprig of cilantro and a lettuce leaf.

Fold the bottom half of the rice wrapper over the filling. Holding the roll firmly in place, fold in the sides of the wrapper. Then, pressing down firmly to hold the folds in place, roll up to close the top.

Repeat with remaining wrappers, shrimp, cilantro and lettuce. Store in an airtight container in the refrigerator until ready to serve (up to 4 hours).

Serve with Vietnamese Dipping Sauce and Peanut Sauce.

Note: Rice noodles and rice paper wrappers are available at Asian markets and in the international section of some supermarkets.

Vietnamese Dipping Sauce

MAKES ABOUT 1 CUP

- ¼ cup fish sauce (see Note)
- ¼ cup sugar
- ¼ cup water
- 3 tablespoons lime juice
- 1 tablespoon vinegar
- 1 garlic clove, crushed
- 1 tablespoon shredded carrot (optional)
  Chili pepper, sliced into rounds
  (optional)

Mix fish sauce, sugar, water, lime juice
and vinegar until sugar dissolves. Adjust
seasoning, adding more lime juice if too
sweet, more sugar if too sour or more fish
sauce if it needs more salt. Stir in garlic.

Add carrot and chili pepper, if desired. Let
stand 30 minutes for flavors to mingle.

Note: Fish sauce is available at Asian
markets and in the international section of
some supermarkets.

Peanut Sauce

MAKES ABOUT ¾ CUP

- ½ cup water
- 2 tablespoons hoisin sauce
- 2 tablespoons peanut butter
  (crunchy or smooth)
- 1 tablespoon sugar
- 1 teaspoon chili paste (see Note)
- ¼ teaspoon garlic powder

Combine all ingredients in a small saucepan over low heat. Whisk until smooth.
Add a little more water if mixture is too
thick. Bring to a boil. Remove from heat.
Cool.

Note: Chili paste is available at Asian
markets and in the international section of
some supermarkets.

MAKES 4 TO 6 SERVINGS

Marty McGreevy of Market Blooms has a passion for Charleston, South Carolina, and has traveled there for the last dozen or so years. This is one of her favorite recipes from the Lowcountry region, though she admits it's more of a technique than an actual recipe. She likes to serve fried green tomatoes with Montrachet (a soft fresh goat cheese) and chopped pecans or a drizzle of aged balsamic vinegar such as Saba.

3 or 4 green tomatoes
  Kosher salt
  Vegetable oil for frying
  All-purpose flour for dusting
2 eggs, beaten well
2 cups panko (see Note)

Cut tomatoes into 1-inch thick slices. Stir 2 tablespoons salt into 2 cups water. Add tomato slices. Soak 15 minutes. Drain. Pat dry with paper towels.

Pour enough oil into a skillet to reach a depth of 1 inch. Heat over medium-high heat.

Place flour in a shallow dish, eggs in another dish and panko in a third dish. Dust the tomatoes with flour, dip in egg, then coat in panko. Working in batches, add tomatoes to skillet. Fry until golden brown, turning once. Transfer tomatoes to paper towels to drain. Repeat with remaining tomatoes, adding more oil to skillet as necessary.

Note: Panko are Japanese bread crumbs available at Asian markets and in the international section of many supermarkets. If you can't find them, dry bread crumbs will work, but the coating won't be as crispy.

Pam's Popcorn Party Mix

MAKES ABOUT 15 CUPS

Pam Tylka of Pam's Market Popcorn also recommends tossing chopped fresh herbs into freshly popped popcorn, then adding a handful of grated Parmesan cheese and butter or olive oil.

6   cups buttered popcorn
6   cups cheddar popcorn
3   cups pretzels
1   cup nuts (any kind)
½   cup (1 stick) butter, melted
¼   cup sweet-hot mustard (such as Ben's)

Combine popcorn, pretzels and nuts. Whisk butter and mustard together to blend. Drizzle over popcorn mixture. Toss to coat.

MAKES 12 TO 18 SERVINGS

Forget sweet cheesecake. This savory cheesecake from CaJohn's Flavor and Fire is a great party appetizer.

1   cup crushed tortilla chips
½   cup (1 stick) butter, melted
2   packages (8 ounces each) cream cheese, softened
1   container (16 ounces) sour cream
2   eggs
2   cups shredded Mexican cheese blend
½   cup chopped green onions
2   garlic cloves, minced
¼   teaspoon ground black pepper
1   jar (16 ounces) CaJohn's Fruit or Berry Salsa

Preheat oven to 350 degrees.

Mix tortilla chips and butter in a bowl. Press onto the bottom of a 9-inch springform pan. Place the pan in a shallow baking dish.

Combine cream cheese, sour cream and eggs in a bowl. Beat with an electric mixer until well blended. Stir in cheese blend, onions, garlic and pepper. Pour mixture into springform pan.

Bake 30 minutes or until a knife inserted in the center comes out clean. Cool completely on a wire rack. Cover and refrigerate 3 hours.

Remove pan sides. Top cheesecake with salsa. Cut into wedges.

4/ $1.00

MAKES 4 TO 6 SERVINGS

One of the things Kevin Eigel grows at his organic farm called Just This Farm is Japanese cucumbers, which are similar to English cucumbers. Here's a recipe that showcases these cukes, though regular cucumbers can be used too.

⅔ cup rice vinegar, white wine vinegar or apple cider vinegar
⅓ cup sugar
    Pinch of salt
3 cups thinly sliced Japanese cucumbers or other cucumbers
2 red or white onions, thinly sliced
    A few dill sprigs or fennel tops
3 tablespoons olive oil

Mix vinegar, sugar and salt in a bowl. Set aside, stirring occasionally until sugar dissolves.

Combine cucumbers, onions and dill sprigs in a large bowl. Add oil to the vinegar mixture. Pour over vegetables. Toss well, then drain, using your hands to squeeze out as much liquid as possible from the vegetables. Cover and refrigerate 1 day before serving.

Bread Salad

This recipe from David Diller of Omega Artisan Baking makes good use of day-old French bread.

1   loaf country French bread, cut into bite-size cubes
20 fresh basil leaves
1   pint grape tomatoes, halved
½   pound green or black olives, pitted
½   cup Balsamic Vinaigrette (recipe follows)
¼   cup shredded Parmesan cheese
    Sea salt and pepper

Mix all ingredients just before serving.

Balsamic Vinaigrette

MAKES ABOUT ¾ CUP

This recipe makes more than you will need for the bread salad, but it will keep in the refrigerator up to a week and can be used on any salad.

½   cup extra-virgin olive oil
¼   cup balsamic vinegar
1   tablespoon crushed garlic
1   tablespoon chopped fresh rosemary
½   teaspoon ground black pepper
¼   teaspoon salt

Whisk all ingredients until well blended.

MAKES 4 SERVINGS

"This is so good, your guests won't believe what's in it," said Mike Kast, owner of Curds and Whey.

½ cup (1 stick) unsalted butter
1 head Boston Bibb or butter lettuce, washed, spun dry
2 tablespoons fresh lemon juice
½ teaspoon coarse salt
Freshly ground black pepper

Melt butter slowly in a saucepan until it starts to bubble. Remove from heat. Skim off whatever solids come to the top. Pour the clarified butter into a small container, leaving the milky residue at the bottom of the pan. Cool to lukewarm.

Place lettuce in a large bowl. Drizzle with clarified butter. Toss. Add lemon juice, salt and pepper. Toss again. Serve immediately.

Corn Chowder

MAKES 6 SERVINGS

Kay Davenport, owner of North Market Cookware, shared this recipe from Kuhn Rikon, one of the suppliers of the cookware and gadgets in her stall. It's a fabulous recipe for summertime when fresh corn is at its peak. A corn zipper, made by Kuhn Rikon, makes quick work of separating the corn kernels from the cob.

8   large ears fresh corn, shucked
1   tablespoon unsalted butter
2   large leeks, white and light green parts only, coarsely chopped
    Salt
4   cups milk or more as needed
4   cups water
3   garlic cloves, pressed
1   jalapeño pepper, seeded, ribs removed, finely chopped (optional)
1   large potato, peeled, cut into small cubes
1   bay leaf
1   tablespoon finely chopped fresh thyme
    Freshly ground black pepper
    Sour cream
    Thinly sliced radish or jalapeño pepper (optional)

Working over a bowl, cut the corn kernels from the cobs. You should have 6 cups of kernels. Reserve the cobs.

In a heavy 5-quart pot, melt butter over medium heat. Add leeks. Season with salt. Cook until leeks have softened, about 5 minutes. Add corn cobs, milk, water, garlic, jalapeño (if using), potato, bay leaf and thyme. Increase heat to high. Bring to a boil. Season to taste with salt and pepper. Reduce heat. Partially cover pot and simmer 30 minutes.

Remove and discard corn cobs. Add corn kernels. Increase heat and cook until corn is tender, about 5 minutes. If soup is too thick, thin with a little milk. Adjust seasoning if necessary.

Ladle soup into bowls. Garnish with a dollop of sour cream and a few slices of radish or jalapeño, if desired.

MAKES 6 SERVINGS

This recipe is from Dareen Wearstler of Better Earth. "This is my sister Fran's favorite recipe from Baton Rouge," she said.

3   tablespoons olive oil
2   tablespoons Creole or spicy brown mustard
2   tablespoons red wine vinegar
1   tablespoon minced green onion
1   teaspoon sugar
⅛ to ¼ teaspoon cayenne pepper
1   bag (16 ounces) shredded cole slaw mix or 8 cups shredded cabbage
1   can (14 ounces) quartered artichoke hearts, drained, coarsely chopped
1   jar (7 ounces) pimiento-stuffed manzanilla or other green olives, drained

In a large bowl, combine oil, mustard, vinegar, onion, sugar and cayenne. Mix well.

Add cabbage, artichokes and olives. Toss well.

Cover and chill at least 1 hour and up to 1 day.

Heirloom Tomato and Bread Soup

MAKES 4 TO 6 SERVINGS

This recipe from James and Karin Barr at Quiverfull Family Farm is a great way to use stale bread.

2	tablespoons olive oil
1	large yellow onion, diced
4	garlic cloves, minced
2	teaspoons fresh thyme leaves
8	cups diced heirloom tomatoes (about 10 medium)
2	tablespoons balsamic vinegar
1	teaspoon sugar
4	cups slightly stale, good-quality bread cubes
	Salt and freshly ground black pepper
½	cup fresh basil leaves, torn
¼	cup grated Parmesan cheese

Heat oil in a large pot. Add onion. Sauté, stirring often, until just tender, about 4 minutes. Add garlic and thyme. Sauté another 2 minutes. Add tomatoes, vinegar and sugar. Bring to a simmer, stirring frequently. Stir in bread.

Cover pot and remove from heat. Let stand 20 minutes. Uncover pot and stir well to break up the bread. Season to taste with salt and pepper. Stir in basil and cheese.

The soup can be served warm, chilled or hot (just return to a simmer).

MAKES 8 SERVINGS

Think of serving this warming soup from Oakvale Farm as a first course or light lunch on a cold winter day.

- 6   bacon slices, cut into 1-inch pieces
- 3   pounds russet potatoes (about 5 large)
- 3½ teaspoons salt
- ½   cup (1 stick) butter
- 1   cup sour cream
- 2⅔ cups whole milk
- ½   teaspoon ground black pepper
- 4   green onions, thinly sliced
- ¾   cup shredded aged or regular Gouda cheese (preferably Oakvale)

Cook bacon in a skillet until crisp. Drain on paper towels. Set aside.

Cut potatoes into thirds. Place in a large pot. Cover with water. Add 2 teaspoons of the salt. Bring to a boil. Reduce heat and simmer until potatoes are very soft, about 45 minutes. Drain.

Return potatoes to the pot and mash with a potato masher until smooth. Add butter and sour cream. Stir until butter melts. Add milk, remaining 1½ teaspoons salt, and pepper. Bring to a simmer (do not boil).

Ladle soup into bowls. Garnish with green onions, Gouda and bacon.

Mushroom Bisque

MAKES 4 TO 6 SERVINGS

This recipe comes from Toby Run Growers, one of the regular farmers at the Saturday farmers' market at the North Market. Toby Run specializes in mushrooms.

⅓ cup margarine
2 cups sliced mushrooms
⅓ cup finely chopped onion
1 teaspoon finely chopped garlic
⅓ cup all-purpose flour
¼ teaspoon ground black pepper
2 cans (14 ounces each) chicken broth
1 cup sliced carrots
2 cups half-and-half
¼ teaspoon cayenne pepper
 Chopped fresh parsley

Melt margarine in a large heavy saucepan. Add mushrooms, onion and garlic. Sauté until tender. Stir in flour and pepper. Cook 1 minute. Add broth and carrots. Cook over medium heat 8 to 10 minutes, stirring frequently. Add half-and-half and cayenne pepper. Cook 7 to 9 minutes longer, stirring frequently.

Ladle into bowls. Sprinkle with parsley.

MAKES ABOUT 6 SERVINGS

This recipe is from Elizabeth Lahmer, the herd veterinarian for Oakvale Farm.

1   bunch broccoli, cut into small pieces
1   head cauliflower, cut into small pieces
1   cup shredded Gouda cheese (preferably Oakvale)
1   cup mayonnaise or Miracle Whip
1   cup sugar
½   cup cashews (optional)
1   tablespoon minced onion

Combine broccoli and cauliflower in a large bowl. Toss to mix. Add all remaining ingredients and mix well. Cover and refrigerate at least 1 hour before serving.

Sweet Potato and Leek Soup

MAKES 4 SERVINGS

This recipe from Dave Bihn of Grapes of Mirth goes wonderfully with hard cider or a Belgian Double Abbey Ale. To make it a vegan soup, use olive oil instead of butter and eliminate the chorizo.

1   quart vegetable broth
1   large sweet potato, roasted, peeled, mashed
1   bay leaf
1½ tablespoons butter or olive oil
2   leeks, sliced (white and pale green parts only)
½   cup bulk Mexican chorizo
½   cup shiitake or other mushrooms, stems removed, caps sliced
1   tablespoon amontillado sherry
    Salt and pepper

Whisk broth and potato together in a large pot. Add bay leaf. Bring to a simmer.

Melt butter in a large skillet. Add leeks. Sauté until soft. Add to potato mixture.

Brown chorizo in the skillet. Using a slotted spoon, transfer chorizo to paper towels to drain. Set aside.

Add mushrooms to drippings in skillet. Sauté until soft. Add sherry. Bring to a boil, scraping up browned bits. Add to pot. Simmer 20 minutes. Season to taste with salt and pepper.

Remove bay leaf from soup. Purée half of the soup in a blender until smooth, then return to pot and stir to blend. (Or, purée all of the soup for a smoother texture.)

Ladle soup into bowls. Sprinkle with chorizo.

Brandied Crab

MAKES 4 SERVINGS

This recipe, from Doug Denny of The Fish Guys, can be served as a main dish or as an appetizer.

2   tablespoons butter or margarine
¼   cup finely chopped fresh parsley
2   tablespoons brandy
    Juice of 1 lemon
⅛   teaspoon nutmeg
⅛   teaspoon paprika
⅛   teaspoon salt
⅛   teaspoon ground white pepper
1   pound backfin crabmeat, picked over
8   slices thinly sliced French bread, toasted

Melt butter in a large skillet. Add parsley, brandy, lemon juice, nutmeg, paprika, salt and pepper. Heat until hot. Add crabmeat. Toss lightly, being careful not to break up lumps of crabmeat.

Arrange bread on plates. Top each slice with a mound of crab mixture.

MAKES 4 SERVINGS

"I like to serve this on steamed greens such as spinach or beet tops," said Doug Denny of The Fish Guys.

- 2   tablespoons balsamic vinegar
- 2   tablespoons extra-virgin olive oil
- 1½ teaspoons peeled and minced fresh ginger
- ½   teaspoon minced garlic
- 1   pound skin-on arctic char fillets
      Olive oil

Preheat broiler.

Whisk vinegar, oil, ginger and garlic in a small bowl.

With a sharp knife, cut a crisscross pattern in the skin side of the char, making cuts ½ inch deep. Baste with olive oil. Arrange skin side up on a broiler pan. Broil until skin is dark brown and fish is cooked through, about 5 to 7 minutes.

Transfer fish to plates, skin side down. Drizzle with vinaigrette.

Gouda and Red Onion Pizza

MAKES 4 TO 6 SERVINGS

This recipe from Oakvale Farm was printed in Midwest Living *magazine. In addition to being a meatless main course, it can also be served as an appetizer (it makes about 12 appetizer servings).*

2	tablespoons olive oil
1	large red onion, halved lengthwise, thinly sliced
1	tablespoon chopped fresh thyme or 1 teaspoon dried thyme, crushed
¼	teaspoon salt
¼	teaspoon freshly ground black pepper
1	tablespoon cornmeal
1	package (10 to 13.8 ounces) refrigerated pizza dough
8	ounces Gouda or Edam cheese, shredded

Preheat oven to 400 degrees.

In a large skillet, heat 1 tablespoon of the oil over medium heat. Add onion. Cook 5 to 7 minutes or until onion is tender but not brown, stirring often. Remove from heat. Stir in thyme, salt and pepper.

Grease a baking sheet. Sprinkle with cornmeal. Pat dough into a 12x8-inch rectangle on the baking sheet. Brush dough with remaining 1 tablespoon oil. Sprinkle dough with cheese to within ½ inch of edges. Spoon onion mixture over cheese.

Bake 12 to 15 minutes or until crust is golden.

MAKES 6 TO 8 SERVINGS

Paneer is an Indian cheese similar to cottage cheese. Here, Flavors of India owner Raj Brar uses well-drained cottage cheese as a substitute. Serve this as a side dish or as a meatless main course.

- 4 pounds spinach, stemmed
  Salt
- 2 to 3 fresh green chili peppers
- 3 tablespoons vegetable oil
- ½ teaspoon cumin seeds
- 8 to 10 garlic cloves, chopped
- 1 tablespoon peeled and chopped fresh ginger
- ½ cup cottage cheese, well drained
- 4 tablespoons heavy cream
- 1 tablespoon fresh lemon juice

Blanch spinach in a large pot of boiling salted water 2 minutes. Drain. Plunge spinach into ice water to stop the cooking process. Drain well. Squeeze out excess water. Place spinach and chili peppers in a food processor and purée.

Heat oil in a large heavy skillet. Add cumin seeds. When seeds begin to change color, add garlic and ginger and sauté for 30 seconds. Stir in spinach purée. Season to taste with salt. When mixture comes to a boil, add cottage cheese and mix well. Stir in cream and lemon juice. Serve hot.

Tortilla Española

This recipe, from Mike Kast of Curds and Whey, is a classic Spanish dish, sort of like an omelet. It can be served as a side dish or as a meatless main course. In addition to being delicious, it will leave you with wonderful potato-flavored oil to use in salads or cooking. Use good-quality, but not expensive, olive oil.

2	pounds Yukon gold potatoes
3	cups olive oil
	Salt
3	eggs
1	tablespoon chopped fresh herbs
8	ounces shredded manchego cheese
½	cup chopped pitted black olives

Wash and peel potatoes, if desired. Cut into slices ½ inch thick.

Heat oil in a large heavy saucepan to 300 degrees. Working in batches, cook potatoes until tender but not browned. Using a slotted spoon, transfer potatoes to paper towels to drain. Lightly season potatoes with salt. Reserve cooking oil.

Whisk eggs with ½ teaspoon salt and herbs.

Heat 2 tablespoons reserved cooking oil in a 10-inch nonstick skillet. (Save remaining cooking oil for another use.) Place about one-third of the potato slices in a layer in the skillet. Sprinkle with half of the cheese and olives. Repeat with another potato layer. Top with remaining cheese and olives, then the remaining potatoes. Pour egg mixture over all. Shake skillet to distribute eggs.

Cook until slightly browned on bottom. Place a platter over the skillet. Using oven mitts, carefully flip skillet and platter so tortilla transfers from the skillet to the platter. Place skillet back on stove, then slide tortilla, uncooked side down, from platter into skillet. Cook until browned.

Carefully turn tortilla onto a serving platter. Cool slightly before cutting into wedges. Serve warm or at room temperature.

Cumin Rice

MAKES 2 TO 3 SERVINGS

Dorothy Beehner, a long-time customer at A Touch of Earth, shared this recipe, which is an excellent accompaniment to pork or salmon dishes. Any leftovers can be frozen or used as filling for stuffed peppers or stuffed squash.

2	tablespoons butter
¼	cup chopped onion
1	teaspoon minced garlic (fresh or from a jar)
½	cup long-grain white rice
2	teaspoons ground cumin
1	cup water or broth
½	cup dried fruit such as raisins, dried cherries or cranberries (optional)
1	bay leaf
	Chopped nuts (optional)

Melt 1 tablespoon of the butter in a small pan. Add onion and garlic. Sauté until softened. Add rice and cumin. Stir to mix thoroughly. Add water, dried fruit if desired, and bay leaf. Bring to a boil. Cover and reduce heat. Simmer 18 to 20 minutes or until rice is tender and liquid is absorbed. Remove from heat. Let stand 5 minutes. Stir in remaining 1 tablespoon butter. Sprinkle with chopped nuts if desired.

MAKES 6 SERVINGS

Dave Bihn, owner of Grapes of Mirth, recommends serving this dish with a red Burgundy or Oregon Pinot Noir. He says this recipe is a great way to use leftovers from a cheese tray. His favorite is a mix of blue and goat cheeses.

- 8   ounces elbow macaroni, bow-tie pasta or choo-choo wheels
-     Salt
- 2   tablespoons butter
- 1   medium onion, chopped
- 2   tablespoons flour
-     Ground black pepper
- 2   cups milk
- 12 to 16 ounces cheese (hard cheeses grated, soft cheeses cut into small pieces)
- 1   tablespoon Frank's Hot Sauce
-     Buttered bread crumbs

Preheat oven to 375 degrees.

Cook pasta in a large pot of boiling salted water until almost tender.

Meanwhile, melt butter in a 3- to 4-quart saucepan. Add onion and sauté until translucent. Add flour, salt and pepper. Cook, stirring often, until flour browns. Stir in milk. Bring to a boil. Boil 1 minute, stirring constantly. Remove from heat. Add cheeses and hot sauce. Stir over low heat until cheeses melt. Add pasta and stir well.

Pour mixture into a 2-quart baking dish. Sprinkle with bread crumbs. Bake until topping is golden brown, about 30 to 45 minutes.

Fast and Easy Cheesy Pasta Alfredo

MAKES 6 SERVINGS

Toni Hume of The Source by Wasserstrom likes how easy and delicious this sauce is. She also recommends serving grilled chicken breast over the pasta.

1   package (8 ounces) cream cheese
¾ to 1 cup grated Parmesan cheese
½   cup (1 stick) butter
2   tablespoons garlic powder or 2 to 3 garlic cloves, minced
2   cups (approximately) milk
⅛   teaspoon ground black pepper
1   pound hot cooked pasta, any shape
    Chopped fresh parsley

Mix cream cheese, Parmesan cheese, butter and garlic powder in a heavy medium saucepan. Heat over medium heat, whisking constantly, until cheeses and butter melt. Add enough milk to thin to desired consistency (you may not need all of the milk). Add pepper.

Serve over pasta. Sprinkle with parsley.

MAKES 4 SERVINGS

This recipe is from Doug Denny of The Fish Guys.

- 2 tablespoons olive oil
- 4 large garlic cloves, sliced
- ½ cup bottled clam juice
- ½ cup dry white wine
- 3 dozen littleneck clams, rinsed
- 4 cups diced tomatoes
- 3 green onions, thinly sliced
- ½ cup fresh basil leaves, sliced
- 12 ounces linguine
- Salt

Heat oil in a large pot over low heat. Add garlic. Cook 3 minutes. Add clam juice and wine. Simmer 5 minutes. Add clams. Cover and steam, shaking pan occasionally until clams open. Transfer clams to a serving bowl, discarding any that do not open. Using the same pot, sauté tomatoes, onions and basil for 5 to 10 minutes. Pour over clams.

Cook pasta in a large pot of boiling salted water until tender but still firm. Drain.

Add pasta to clam mixture. Toss.

Shrimp and Fresh Vegetable Angel Hair Pasta

MAKES 4 TO 6 SERVINGS

This recipe comes from Brett Rhoads of Rhoads Farm. It's one of his favorite recipes.

 2 cups white wine
 4 tablespoons butter
 2 garlic cloves, minced
 ½ teaspoon red pepper flakes
 10 ounces angel hair pasta
   Salt
 2 tablespoons olive oil
 1 cup fresh bicolor sweet corn kernels
 1 red bell pepper, coarsely chopped
 1 small zucchini, coarsely chopped
 6 ounces shrimp, peeled, deveined
   Ground black pepper
 ¼ cup freshly grated Parmesan cheese
 2 tablespoons chopped fresh parsley

In a shallow saucepan, combine wine, butter, garlic and pepper flakes. Bring to a boil. Reduce heat and simmer until liquid is reduced by a third.

Meanwhile, cook pasta in a large pot of boiling salted water until tender but still firm.

While pasta cooks, heat oil in another large saucepan over medium heat. Add corn, bell pepper, zucchini and shrimp. Season to taste with salt and pepper. Cook until shrimp is just cooked through and vegetables are slightly tender.

Drain pasta. Place in a large bowl. Add shrimp mixture and toss. Pour wine mixture over. Top with Parmesan and parsley.

All our Bacon & Hams - No MSG or Nitrates!
*Our Own and/or Local

African Style Goat Stew

This recipe comes from Bluescreek Farm. It calls for a large amount of oil; however, after the stew is made, you can skim the oil from the surface and then use it to cook other meats. Or, you can reduce the amount of oil, if you like.

1   cup olive oil
2   large yellow onions, sliced
¼   cup chopped garlic
¼   cup turmeric
1   tablespoon ground ginger or peeled and grated fresh ginger
1   teaspoon salt
    Pinch of ground black pepper
2   pounds bone-in goat stew meat
1   can (28 ounces) canned beef broth
    Hot cooked rice

Heat oil in a heavy stew pot. Add onions and cook until transparent. Add garlic. Cook 1 minute. Stir in turmeric, ginger, salt and pepper. Add meat. Cook until meat is well coated with spices. Reduce heat. Slowly stir in broth. Cover and simmer at least 1 hour (2 hours is better, but it smells so good you may not be able to wait that long). The oil will separate and the meat and onion mixture will be very thick.

Skim oil from the top of the stew. Drizzle oil over hot cooked rice. Spoon stew over rice.

MAKES 4 SERVINGS

This dish from Flavors of India combines marinated grilled chicken with Makhni gravy.

Chicken:
- 1 chicken, cut into quarters
- 3 tablespoons lemon juice
- 2 teaspoons red chili powder (preferably kashmiri)
  Salt
- 1 cup plain yogurt
- 2 tablespoons minced garlic
- 2 tablespoons peeled and minced fresh ginger
- 2 tablespoons mustard oil (see Note)
- ½ teaspoon garam masala (see Note)
- 2 tablespoons butter

Gravy:
- 2 to 3 tablespoons butter
- 1 tablespoon garam masala (see Note)
- 1 tablespoon minced garlic
- 1 tablespoon peeled and minced fresh ginger
- 1 teaspoon chopped green chilies
- 2 cups tomato purée
- 1 tablespoon red chili powder
  Salt
- 2 tablespoons sugar or honey
- ½ teaspoon dried fenugreek leaves (see Note)
- 1 cup heavy cream

To prepare chicken: Cut slits in the chicken. Combine 1 tablespoon of the lemon juice, 1 teaspoon of the chili powder and salt to taste. Rub into chicken. Let stand at room temperature 30 minutes.

Meanwhile, drain yogurt in a strainer lined with cheesecloth for 15 to 20 minutes. Mix drained yogurt with remaining 2 tablespoons lemon juice, remaining 1 teaspoon chili powder, garlic, ginger, mustard oil and garam masala. Pour marinade over chicken. Cover and refrigerate 3 to 4 hours.

Prepare grill (high heat) or preheat oven to 350 degrees. Remove chicken from marinade; discard marinade. Cook chicken, basting occasionally with butter, until almost cooked through. Transfer to a platter.

To make gravy: Melt butter in a large pan. Add garam masala and cook until it crackles. Add garlic, ginger and green chilies. Cook 2 minutes. Add tomato purée, chili powder, salt and 1 cup water. Bring to a boil. Simmer 10 minutes. Add sugar and fenugreek. Add chicken. Simmer until chicken is cooked through. Stir in cream. Heat through.

Note: Garam masala is a spice blend available at specialty foods stores. Mustard oil and fenugreek leaves are available at Indian markets.

Easy Beef Paprika

MAKES 6 SERVINGS

Toni Hume of The Source by Wasserstrom shared this recipe for a simple dish that is perfect for cold winter nights. "This recipe sounds odd, but we make it all the time. It's so good!" she said.

¼ cup olive oil
2 pounds beef stew meat, cut into 1-inch cubes
1 cup sliced onion
1 to 2 garlic cloves, minced
¾ cup ketchup
2 tablespoons Worcestershire sauce
1 tablespoon brown sugar
2 teaspoons paprika
2 teaspoons salt
½ teaspoon dry mustard
2¼ cups water
2 tablespoons flour
3 cups hot cooked noodles

Heat oil in a large skillet. Add meat, onion and garlic. Cook until the meat is browned. Stir in ketchup, Worcestershire sauce, brown sugar, paprika, salt, mustard and 2 cups of the water. Cover and simmer 2 hours or until the meat is fork tender.

Blend remaining ¼ cup water with flour. Stir gradually into meat mixture. Cook until juices thicken.

Serve over noodles.

MAKES ABOUT 3½ CUPS

Use this recipe from Summer Thyme Farm to rub on meat, chicken or ribs before grilling. It captures the essence of summer.

8   garlic cloves, minced
1   cup chopped fresh basil
1   cup chopped fresh parsley
½   cup chopped fresh chives
½   cup chopped fresh oregano
¼   cup chopped fresh cilantro
2   tablespoons chopped fresh rosemary
2   tablespoons chopped fresh sage
1   tablespoon lime juice
1   tablespoon olive oil
1   tablespoon whole black peppercorns

Put all ingredients in a food processor. Blend to a paste. Place in a sealed container. Refrigerate for about 3 hours.

Lamb Kebabs

This recipe comes from Bluescreek Farm Meats.

- ¼ cup olive oil
- ¼ cup red wine vinegar
- 2 tablespoons fresh lemon juice
- 2 tablespoons water
- 1 garlic clove, minced
- 1 teaspoon dried oregano
- ¼ teaspoon ground black pepper
- 12 ounces boneless lamb leg or shoulder, cut into 1-inch cubes
- 1 small yellow squash or zucchini, cut into slices ¼ inch thick
- 1 red bell pepper, cut into squares

In a medium-size nonreactive bowl, combine oil, vinegar, lemon juice, water, garlic, oregano and pepper. Add lamb. Toss to coat. Cover and refrigerate 4 to 8 hours, stirring occasionally.

Prepare grill (medium-high heat) or preheat broiler.

Thread lamb, squash and bell pepper onto 4 skewers. Grill or broil kebabs 4 to 5 inches from heat about 5 minutes or to desired doneness, turning occasionally.

Lamb with Garlic and Herbs

This staple of French cooking is a favorite of Kay Davenport, owner of North Market Cookware. Kay sometimes roasts the lamb with anchovies on top – but be sure to cut back on the salt if you use that technique.

  1 bone-in leg of lamb (about 6 pounds)
     Garlic cloves, cut into slivers
     Olive oil
     Dried herbes de Provence (or a mixture of rosemary, savory, thyme and marjoram)
1½ tablespoons sea salt
     Freshly ground black pepper

Cut slits all over the lamb. Insert slivers of garlic into the slits. Rub with oil, then herbes de Provence. If time allows, cover with foil and refrigerate 2 to 3 hours to allow the flavors to penetrate the meat. Remove from refrigerator 1 hour before roasting to bring meat to room temperature. Sprinkle with salt and pepper.

Preheat oven to 400 degrees.

Roast lamb 15 minutes. Reduce oven temperature to 350 degrees. Roast until the internal temperature of the lamb is 130 degrees. Let rest 15 minutes before carving.

Stacked Burrito

This recipe from CaJohn's Flavor and Fire is a new twist on traditional burritos.

1 pound ground beef
3 tablespoons CaBoom! Chili Fixins' or other chili seasoning
1 cup water
2 jars (16 ounces each) CaBoom! Picante Sauce or other picante sauce
¼ cup chopped fresh cilantro leaves, plus additional for garnish
2 cans (15 ounces each) refried beans
7 flour tortillas (burrito size)
2 cups shredded Mexican cheese blend

Preheat oven to 400 degrees.

Brown ground beef in a skillet. Drain. Stir in Chili Fixins' and water. Cook until the liquid evaporates. Remove from heat. Stir in a half jar of the picante sauce and ¼ cup cilantro.

Spoon refried beans into a bowl. Stir in a half jar of the picante sauce.

Place 1 tortilla on a baking sheet. Spread with some of the bean mixture to within ½ inch of the edge of tortilla. Top with another tortilla. Spread with some of the meat mixture and ¼ cup of the cheese. Top with another tortilla. Continue alternating beans, tortillas, meat and cheese, ending with bean mixture. Cover with foil.

Bake 40 minutes. Remove foil. Sprinkle with remaining cheese.

Cut into wedges. Garnish with additional cilantro. Serve with remaining jar of picante sauce.

MAKES 10 SERVINGS

Steve Beard of North Market Produce says this is delicious, but he only makes it once a year – for the Super Bowl.

4 tablespoons olive oil	2 tablespoons dried basil
½ pound ground chicken	1 tablespoon garlic powder
6 tablespoons finely chopped garlic	1 tablespoon paprika
1 habanero pepper, minced	2 teaspoons dried oregano
1 jalapeño pepper, minced	2 teaspoons dried rosemary
1 medium onion, chopped	2 teaspoons dried thyme
1 green bell pepper, chopped	Pinch of dried red chili flakes
½ carrot, shredded	2 cans (15 ounces each) stewed tomatoes
½ celery stalk, finely chopped	1 can (27 ounces) cannellini beans, partially drained
1½ cups chicken stock	
4 tablespoons chili powder	1 can (4 ounces) diced green chilies

In a large heavy saucepan, heat 2 tablespoons of the olive oil over medium heat. Add chicken. Sauté, crumbling chicken into small pieces as it cooks, until fully cooked. Using a slotted spoon, transfer chicken to plate.

Heat remaining oil in same pan. Add garlic, habanero and jalapeño. Sauté 2 minutes. Add onion, bell pepper, carrot and celery. Sauté until the vegetables have released their liquid and softened.

Return chicken to pan. Add stock and all seasonings. Taste and adjust seasonings if necessary (it should be quite spicy). Add tomatoes, beans and canned chilies. Bring to a boil. Reduce heat and simmer 45 minutes to 1 hour.

Tartiflette

MAKES 4 MAIN-COURSE OR 8 SIDE-DISH SERVINGS

"I received this recipe from a French customer," said Mike Kast, owner of Curds and Whey. "I first served it on New Year's Day, and it garnered rave reviews from all of my friends. I believe it is a candidate for the best dish of all time."

Kast notes that this is a country dish so amounts and proportions can be varied as you wish. However, to call it a tartiflette, *it must be made with Reblochon. If you use stock instead of cream, the dish will be less rich but the ingredients will shine. If you use cream, the dish will be more luscious but less intense.*

- 3 pounds Yukon gold potatoes
- 1 quart chicken stock or cream
  Salt and pepper
- ½ pound bacon, cut into small pieces
- 1 cup chopped onion
- 1 wheel Reblochon cheese *(fromage de Savoie),* cut in half lengthwise

Preheat oven to 350 degrees.

Peel potatoes, if you like, and cut into ½-inch rounds.

Heat stock or cream to a simmer. Add potatoes, ½ teaspoon salt and pepper to taste. Cook until potatoes are tender but firm.

Meanwhile, cook bacon in a skillet until fat is rendered. Add onion and cook until softened. Spoon bacon mixture into a gratin dish.

Using a slotted spoon, carefully spoon potatoes over bacon mixture, leaving liquid behind. Place cheese, rind side up, over potatoes.

Bake until bubbly and cheese rind is browned, about 25 minutes. Let stand 10 minutes before serving.

MAKES 4 SERVINGS

Pam Tylka of Pam's Market Popcorn has found interesting uses for popcorn, including using it as a crust for chicken.

Thai Peanut Sauce:
- 3 tablespoons honey
- 3 tablespoons peanut butter
- 2 tablespoons lime juice
- 2 tablespoons soy sauce
- ½ teaspoon hot pepper sauce

Chicken:
- 2 cups popped popcorn
- ½ cup chopped peanuts
- 1 egg
- 1 garlic clove, minced
- 1 teaspoon soy sauce
- ½ teaspoon hot pepper sauce
- 3 tablespoons vegetable oil
- 4 boneless skinless chicken breasts (about 1¾ pounds total)

To make the sauce: Combine all ingredients in a small bowl. Stir until smooth.

To prepare chicken: Preheat oven to 350 degrees.

Process popped popcorn in a food processor until ground. Pour popcorn into a shallow dish. Stir in peanuts.

In another shallow dish, whisk egg, garlic, soy sauce and hot pepper sauce until blended.

Heat oil in a large ovenproof skillet over medium-high heat. Dip chicken into the egg mixture, then into the popcorn mixture, turning to coat well. Place chicken in skillet. Cook until browned on both sides, about 3 minutes per side. Transfer skillet to oven. Bake until chicken is cooked through, about 15 minutes.

Serve chicken with Thai Peanut Sauce.

MAKES 4 SERVINGS

This recipe is from Sarah Karlsberger at The Archive. She says it's "the" grilled chicken sandwich, in part because many of the ingredients can be found at the North Market. Of course, if you don't live in Columbus, you can find good substitutions at your local farmers' market and bakeries.

¼ cup slaw dressing (such as Marzetti) plus additional for spreading on rolls
2 to 3 tablespoons tamari soy sauce
4 boneless skinless chicken breasts (preferably from North Market Poultry)
   Olive oil
4 cheddar-scallion rolls (from Omega Artisan Baking)
   Honey mustard (such as Ingelhoffer)
   Roasted Garlic Cheddar Cheese (from Curds and Whey), thinly sliced
   Fresh pesto sauce (from Pastaria)

Preheat oven to 325 degrees.

Mix slaw dressing and soy sauce. Pour over chicken breasts. Set aside to marinate.

Heat a large skillet (preferably cast iron) over high heat. Add a small amount of olive oil. Drain marinade from the chicken. Working in batches, add chicken to skillet. Cook until brown, about 1 minute per side. Transfer chicken to a baking dish. Bake until cooked through, about 25 minutes. (Chicken can be prepared ahead. Cool, then cover and refrigerate.)

When ready to serve, heat a skillet over medium-high heat.

Cut off the tops and bottoms of the rolls (save for bread crumbs for another use). Cut rolls in half horizontally. Brush 1 cut side of each slice very lightly with slaw dressing. Place half of the rolls, slaw dressing side down, in skillet. Top with mustard, chicken breast, cheese and pesto. Top with other half of rolls, slaw dressing side up. Grill until golden brown on both sides, turning once.

Applesauce Muffins

MAKES 2 DOZEN

This recipe from Jim and Karin Barr of Quiverfull Family Farm makes good use of their stone-ground wheat flour.

1	cup sugar
½	cup shortening
2	eggs
1	cup applesauce
2	cups stone-ground whole wheat flour
3	teaspoons baking powder
½	teaspoon baking soda

Preheat oven to 375 degrees. Grease 24 muffin cups.

Cream sugar and shortening in a mixing bowl. Mix in eggs and applesauce.

In a separate bowl, stir together flour, baking powder and soda. Add to creamed mixture, stirring only enough to moisten the dry ingredients.

Spoon batter into prepared muffin cups, filling each ⅔ full. Bake 20 to 25 minutes. Serve warm.

MAKES ABOUT 16 SERVINGS

"I've been holding on to the same scrap of paper with this recipe from our former neighbor for 30 years," said Sarah Karlsberger of The Archive. "It's easy and beautiful every time."

½ cup finely chopped pecans
¼ cup sugar
2 tablespoons cinnamon
2 cups superfine granulated sugar (see Note)
1 cup (2 sticks) butter
1 cup sour cream
2 eggs
1 teaspoon vanilla extract
2 cups all-purpose flour
1 teaspoon baking powder
¼ teaspoon salt

Preheat oven to 350 degrees. Grease and flour a bundt pan.

Combine pecans, sugar and cinnamon.

Cream superfine sugar, butter, sour cream, eggs and vanilla. Sift together flour, baking powder and salt. Stir dry ingredients into butter mixture by hand (batter will be very thick).

Sprinkle a third of the pecan mixture in the bottom of prepared pan. Spoon in about half of the batter. Smooth out. Repeat layers again, then top with remaining pecan mixture.

Bake until a toothpick inserted near the center comes out clean, about 1 hour. Cool cake in pan on rack 15 to 30 minutes. Turn cake out onto platter.

Note: Superfine sugar is available at gourmet markets and in the baking section of some supermarkets. If you can't find it, whirl regular granulated sugar in a food processor until finely ground.

Raspberry Cornmeal Muffins

MAKES 18

Raspberry season in Ohio is wonderful in part because it's so short. I developed this recipe using fresh raspberries. The muffins aren't too sweet, and the cornmeal adds a lovely texture.

1   cup yellow cornmeal
1   cup all-purpose flour
½   cup sugar
1   teaspoon baking powder
1   teaspoon baking soda
¼   teaspoon salt
2   large eggs
1½ cups plain yogurt
¼   cup (½ stick) unsalted butter, melted, cooled
1   cup fresh raspberries

Preheat oven to 400 degrees. Line muffin cups with foil or paper liners.

Combine cornmeal, flour, sugar, baking powder, soda and salt in a large bowl. Mix using a whisk. In another bowl, whisk eggs, yogurt and butter. Add wet ingredients to dry ingredients. Stir just until mixed. Gently fold in raspberries.

Divide batter among prepared muffin cups. Bake until golden and a tester inserted in the center comes out clean, about 15 to 20 minutes.

Cool muffins in cups 5 minutes. Turn muffins out onto racks to cool.

MAKES 12 TO 16 SERVINGS

"This is a moist, delicious coffeecake that will bring in family and friends every time," said Toni Hume of The Source by Wasserstrom. The cake can also be frozen.

Cake:
 3   cups flour
1½ teaspoons baking powder
1½ teaspoons baking soda
¼   teaspoon salt
1½ cups (3 sticks) butter, room temperature
1½ cups sugar
 3   eggs
1½ cups sour cream
1½ teaspoons vanilla

Filling:
 1   cup brown sugar
¾   cup chopped pecans (optional)
 2   teaspoons cinnamon

Preheat oven to 325 degrees. Grease and flour a 13x9-inch pan.

To make cake: Blend flour, baking powder, soda and salt.

Beat butter and sugar until fluffy. Add eggs 1 at a time. Blend in sour cream and vanilla. Gradually add the dry ingredients. Mix well.

To make filling: Combine brown sugar, pecans and cinnamon in a small bowl.

To assemble: Pour half of the batter into prepared pan. Sprinkle half of the filling over batter. Top with remaining batter. Sprinkle with remaining filling.

Bake 45 to 60 minutes. If cake browns too fast, cover with foil.

The Easiest Focaccia

MAKES ABOUT 15 SERVINGS

"All you need is a bowl, something to stir with and some imagination." That's how Amy Lozier, owner and baker of Omega Artisan Baking, describes this recipe. For toppings, you can use anything from the simplest ingredients – sea salt and olive oil – to selections that result in more of a meal – sliced tomatoes, olives, salami. Lozier cautions against using anything that might burn, such as whole fresh basil leaves.

4 cups bread flour or all-purpose flour

2½ teaspoons instant yeast or 3¼ teaspoons active dry yeast

1 tablespoon plus 2 teaspoons kosher salt, or 1 tablespoon table salt, plus additional for sprinkling

2 cups water, at room temperature

Nonstick cooking spray

Cornmeal

Olive oil

Toppings of choice

In a large bowl, combine 2½ cups of the flour, yeast, salt and water. Stir with a wooden spoon until mixture is smooth. Stir in remaining flour, ½ cup at a time, until the dough starts to pull away from the sides of the bowl. This is a wet dough; you can sprinkle with more flour if it's too sticky.

Cover bowl with plastic wrap. Let dough rest at room temperature 40 to 60 minutes until it is doubled in volume. (Or, the dough can be refrigerated overnight. Remove from refrigerator 1½ to 2 hours before you want to use it.)

Preheat the oven to its highest setting (500 degrees to 550 degrees). Place a pizza stone in the oven to preheat. Cut a piece of parchment paper the size of a cookie sheet and place on the back of a cookie sheet turned upside-down. Mist parchment with nonstick cooking spray, then sprinkle with cornmeal. Set aside.

Turn the dough out onto an oiled counter. Oil your fingers too. Pull and stretch the dough to the size of the parchment paper. Lift dough carefully and place on parchment. Add toppings of your choice. Be sure to sprinkle with some salt. Dimple the dough by pressing with your fingertips.

Lift the cookie sheet and slide the dough and parchment onto the pizza stone. Immediately turn the oven temperature down to 400 degrees. Bake 25 to 40 minutes, depending on the thickness of the dough.

Note: If you don't have a pizza stone, oil a pan (any shape) and place it in the oven to preheat. Slide the dough and parchment onto the pan when ready to bake.

MAKES 3 SMALL LOAVES

This recipe comes from Heil Family Deli. It's a great way to use the abundance of zucchini available in the summer.

2½ cups sugar
 1 cup vegetable oil
 3 eggs
 2 cups grated zucchini
 3 teaspoons vanilla
 3 cups flour
 3 teaspoons cinnamon
 1 teaspoon baking soda
 ½ teaspoon salt
 ¼ teaspoon baking powder
    Chopped nuts (optional)
    Raisins (optional)

Preheat oven to 350 degrees. Butter 3 small loaf pans.

Blend sugar and oil well. Add eggs 1 at a time, beating well after each addition. Stir in zucchini and vanilla.

Sift flour, cinnamon, soda, salt and baking powder into a large bowl. Add to zucchini mixture. Stir in nuts and/or raisins, if desired.

Divide batter among prepared pans. Bake 50 to 60 minutes or until a toothpick inserted in the center comes out clean.

MAKES ABOUT 16 SERVINGS

"This cake is infamous at our house," said Sarah Karlsberger of *The Archive*, who jokingly calls the recipe *"Friends Don't Let Friends Eat Cake and Drive Cake."*

5	ounces unsweetened chocolate, chopped	1	cup (2 sticks) butter
2	cups sifted all-purpose flour	2	cups superfine sugar (see Note)
1	teaspoon baking soda	1	teaspoon vanilla extract
¼	teaspoon salt	3	eggs
¼	cup instant coffee powder		Chopped pecans (optional)
½	cup bourbon		Additional bourbon (optional)
			Confectioners' sugar

Preheat oven to 325 degrees. Grease and flour a 10-cup bundt pan.

Place chocolate in the top of a double boiler over low heat. Stir until chocolate melts and is smooth. Remove from heat. Cool slightly.

Sift flour, soda and salt.

In a 2-cup glass measuring cup, dissolve coffee in a bit of boiling water. Add cold water to reach the 1½ cups line. Add bourbon.

Cream butter in a large bowl with an electric mixer. Add sugar and vanilla. Beat until smooth. Add eggs 1 at a time, beating well after each addition. Beat in chocolate. With mixer on low speed, alternately add dry ingredients and coffee mixture to batter, scraping bowl frequently. Beat until smooth (batter will be thin).

Pour batter into prepared pan, layering with pecans, if desired. Bake until toothpick inserted near center comes out clean, about 1 hour 15 minutes.

Transfer pan to rack and cool about 15 minutes. Turn cake out onto rack to cool completely. Sprinkle with additional bourbon, if desired. When ready to serve, dust with confectioners' sugar.

Note: Superfine sugar is available at gourmet stores and in the baking section of some supermarkets. If you can't find it, whirl granulated sugar in a food processor until finely ground.

Chocolate Pâte

MAKES 10 SERVINGS

Daniel Cooper of Pure Imagination Chocolatier gives pâte a new twist by turning it into an indulgent chocolate dessert.

- 1   cup (2 sticks) butter
- 3   cups semisweet chocolate chips
- 1   teaspoon instant coffee crystals, crushed
- ½   cup sugar
- 2   eggs (see Note)
- 1   teaspoon vanilla
- 1½ cups whipping cream

Line a loaf pan with plastic wrap.

Melt butter in a heavy medium saucepan over medium-low heat. Add chocolate and coffee crystals. Stir until chocolate melts and mixture is smooth. Pour into a large bowl. Add sugar. Beat well. Add eggs and vanilla. Beat well.

In another bowl, beat cream with clean dry beaters until stiff peaks form. Fold into chocolate mixture.

Pour chocolate mixture into prepared pan. Cover loosely. Refrigerate overnight.

Remove pâte from pan. Remove plastic. Cut into slices.

Note: This recipe contains raw eggs. There is a small chance of salmonella poisoning when consuming raw eggs.

MAKES 12 SERVINGS

Jim and Karin Barr have just started growing blackberries and raspberries at Quiverfull Family Farm. This recipe showcases the delicate summer fruit.

1	cup (2 sticks) butter
1½	cups flour
1	cup confectioners' sugar
8	ounces cream cheese, softened
¼	cup milk
4	cups fresh blackberries
1¾	cups granulated sugar
½	cup water
6	tablespoons cornstarch
12	ounces whipped topping

Preheat oven to 350 degrees.

Melt butter. Mix with flour. Press into a 13x9-inch baking dish. Bake 20 minutes. Cool.

Beat confectioners' sugar, cream cheese and milk. Pour over cooled crust.

In a medium saucepan, mix blackberries, granulated sugar, water and cornstarch. Bring to a boil. Cook 3 minutes. Cool. Pour over cream cheese layer, spreading evenly. Cover with whipped topping. Refrigerate until set.

Grandma's Caramel Corn

MAKES ABOUT 8 SERVINGS

This recipe is from Dave Bihn of Grapes of Mirth.

5	quarts hot popped popcorn (do not use microwave popcorn)
2	cups brown sugar
½	cup (1 stick) butter or margarine
½	cup light corn syrup
	Pinch of cream of tartar
1	teaspoon baking soda

Preheat oven to 200 degrees. Keep popcorn warm in oven.

Mix brown sugar, butter, corn syrup and cream of tartar in a 4-quart saucepan. Bring to a boil over medium heat, stirring often. Boil 5 minutes. Remove from heat. Add soda. Mix well. Pour over popcorn and toss to coat.

Transfer mixture to a lightly greased baking sheet. Bake 1 hour, stirring every 15 minutes.

MAKES 4 SERVINGS

This recipe from Jeni Britton of Jeni's Ice Cream makes a lot of brandied cherries, which will last for a few weeks if stored in the refrigerator. They are good as an ice cream topping on their own.

Brandied Cherries:
- 1 pound black cherries (frozen are great)
- ¼ cup brandy
- ¼ cup sugar

Honey and Vin Santo Sauce:
- ¼ cup Vin Santo (or other dessert wine)
- 2 tablespoons honey

Honeyed Whipped Cream:
- 2 teaspoons honey
- 1 cup heavy cream

Salty Caramel ice cream

To make brandied cherries: Combine cherries, brandy and sugar in a saucepan. Bring to a boil. Boil 5 minutes. Cool. (Refrigerate overnight if possible.)

To make sauce: Combine Vin Santo and honey in a small saucepan. Heat until warm. Remove from heat.

To make whipped cream: Pour honey into a medium bowl. Add a splash of cream. Mix until honey is thoroughly incorporated. Add remaining cream. Beat until soft peaks form.

To assemble: Scoop Salty Caramel ice cream into bowls. Drizzle with Honey and Vin Santo Sauce. Top with Honeyed Whipped Cream and a few Brandied Cherries.

Jeni's Amazing Vanilla Bean Caramel Sauce

MAKES ABOUT 5 CUPS

"OK, I'll give you the recipe that I've worked years to perfect," said Jeni Britton, owner of Jeni's Fresh Ice Creams. "I don't mind. This caramel sauce is the best I've ever had. We serve it warm at our shops. Don't skimp on the salt!"

1	quart heavy cream
1	vanilla bean, split lengthwise
½	pound (1 cup plus 2 tablespoons) dark brown sugar
½	pound (1 cup plus 2 tablespoons) light brown sugar
2	teaspoons vanilla extract
	Pinch of sea salt

Pour cream into a heavy saucepan. Scrape seeds from vanilla bean into the cream. Add the bean and both sugars. Bring to a boil over medium heat, stirring until sugar dissolves. Boil 8 minutes. Pour into another container. Add vanilla and salt. Stir to blend. Remove vanilla bean.

The sauce will be thick when cool and thin when warm. Reheat in the top of a double boiler or microwave gently.

MAKES 1 TO 2 DOZEN

This recipe, named for the Austrian city of Linz, is from Mariana Chambers of Mozart's Bakery.

1   **cup (2 sticks) butter, softened**
⅔   **cup sugar**
2   **eggs, separated**
1   **teaspoon vanilla extract**
    Zest of 1 lemon
2½ **cups all-purpose flour**
½   **teaspoon cinnamon**
¼   **teaspoon salt**
½   **cup almonds, ground, finely chopped or sliced**
½   **cup black currant, raspberry or other jam or preserves**

In a large mixing bowl, cream butter and sugar by hand. Beat in egg yolks, vanilla and lemon zest.

Combine flour, cinnamon and salt. Add to butter mixture. Mix by hand only long enough to gather dough together. (Do not overwork or cookies will be tough.) Shape into a loaf. Wrap in plastic. Refrigerate at least 1 hour and up to several days.

Preheat oven to 350 degrees. Grease cookie sheets or line with parchment.

On a lightly floured surface, roll dough to ⅛- to ¼-inch thickness. Cut out rounds of dough with a 2- or 3-inch cookie cutter. Cut out the centers of half of the rounds using a smaller round cookie cutter. Reroll the scraps once and cut out more cookies.

Lightly beat egg whites. Brush egg whites over rounds with centers cut out, then pat almonds onto them. Alternately, you could sprinkle rounds lightly with sugar. Arrange all rounds on prepared cookie sheets.

Bake 12 to 20 minutes or until lightly browned. Transfer cookies to wire racks and cool completely.

Spread a thin layer of jam on plain cookies, then top with almond-coated cookies, creating sandwiches (the jam will show through the hole).

Mozart's Cinnamon Bread Pudding

MAKES ABOUT 12 SERVINGS

This recipe from Mozart's Bakery is a wonderful way to use day-old cinnamon bread. This dessert is also delicious for breakfast; instead of lemon sauce, serve with maple syrup.

Bread Pudding:
- 1 loaf cinnamon bread, cut into cubes
- 2¼ cups half-and-half
- 2 eggs
- ¼ cup sugar
- 1 teaspoon vanilla
- ½ teaspoon salt

Lemon Sauce:
- ½ cup sugar
- 1 tablespoon cornstarch
- Pinch of nutmeg
- Pinch of salt
- 1 cup boiling water
- 2 tablespoons butter
- 1½ tablespoons lemon juice

To make Bread Pudding: Butter a shallow glass baking dish, about 12x9 inches. Arrange bread cubes in dish.

In a mixing bowl, combine half-and-half, eggs, sugar, vanilla and salt. Whisk to mix. Pour over bread cubes, stirring gently to coat. Let stand while preheating oven to 350 degrees.

Bake 30 to 45 minutes.

To make Lemon Sauce: Mix sugar, cornstarch, nutmeg and salt in a saucepan. Stir in water. Cook over low heat, stirring, until mixture is thick and clear. Blend in butter and lemon juice.

Spread over bread pudding.

MAKES ABOUT 12 SERVINGS

This recipe from Heil Family Deli is a favorite around the holidays.

Cake:
- 2   cups sugar
- 4   eggs
- 1   cup vegetable oil
- 2   cups flour
- 2   teaspoons baking soda
- 2   teaspoons cinnamon
- ½   teaspoon salt
- 2   cups canned pumpkin (not pumpkin pie filling)
- 2   teaspoons vanilla

Icing:
- 1   box (16 ounces) confectioners' sugar
- 8   ounces cream cheese
- 1   cup nuts
- ½   cup (1 stick) butter
- 1   teaspoon vanilla

Preheat oven to 350 degrees. Butter and flour two 8- or 9-inch round cake pans or loaf pans.

To make cake: Beat sugar and eggs until well blended. Beat in oil. Add flour, soda, cinnamon and salt. Beat well. Beat in pumpkin and vanilla.

Divide batter between pans. Bake 35 minutes. Turn cakes out onto racks to cool.

To make icing: Combine confectioners' sugar, cream cheese, nuts, butter and vanilla. Beat until well blended. Spread over cake.

Triple Ginger Pecan Biscotti

MAKES 2 TO 3 DOZEN COOKIES

These biscotti from A Touch of Earth have a wonderfully complex flavor. They are not very sweet so they're especially good paired with ice cream. They are also excellent as an appetizer with wine or after a meal with a dessert wine.

½   cup sugar
¼   cup (½ stick) butter, softened
1½ cups coarsely chopped toasted pecans
¾   cup minced crystallized ginger
2   tablespoons ground ginger
1   tablespoon peeled and grated fresh ginger
2   medium eggs
1½ cups all-purpose flour
¾   teaspoon baking powder
2   tablespoons turbinado sugar (optional)

Preheat oven to 375 degrees. Line a baking sheet with parchment or spray with nonstick cooking spray.

Cream sugar and butter. Stir in pecans, crystallized ginger, ground ginger, fresh ginger and eggs.

In a small bowl, combine flour and baking powder. Add to butter mixture. Divide dough into halves or thirds. On a well-floured surface, with your hands slightly dampened, shape each portion of dough into a log. Transfer logs to prepared baking sheet. Sprinkle with turbinado sugar, if desired.

Bake until logs are firm and brown, about 20 minutes. Cool on a rack 5 to 10 minutes.

Slice logs diagonally into ¾-inch-thick slices. Return slices to baking sheet, cut side down. Bake 15 to 20 minutes to desired degree of crispness (biscotti will be slightly crisper after cooling). Transfer biscotti to racks. Cool completely.

MAKES 2 PIES

Kevin Eigel of Just This Farm makes this twist on traditional pumpkin pie. "Winter squash is naturally sweeter and more flavorful than pumpkin," he says.

2½	cups mashed steamed or baked winter squash (such as butternut or acorn)
½	cup honey or maple syrup
1	teaspoon lemon extract
½	teaspoon cinnamon
½	teaspoon ground ginger
½	teaspoon nutmeg
½	teaspoon salt
4	eggs, slightly beaten
1½	cups half-and-half
2	(9-inch) pie crusts

Preheat oven to 425 degrees.

In a mixing bowl, combine squash, honey, lemon extract, cinnamon, ginger, nutmeg and salt. Mix well. Add eggs to squash mixture. Gradually mix in half-and-half. Divide mixture between crusts.

Bake 15 minutes. Reduce oven temperature to 350 degrees. Bake 45 minutes.

MAKES 1 SERVING

This recipe is from Bubbles: The Tea and Juice Company. While bubble tea, made with tapioca pearls, is a specialty, owner Eric Ling also makes smoothies and other drinks such as this one.

1½ cups ice cubes
 2 tablespoons almond milk
 1 tablespoon sweetened condensed milk

Combine all ingredients in a blender. Process until smooth. Serve immediately.

Aztec Hot Chocolate

MAKES ABOUT 2 SERVINGS

Daniel Cooper of Pure Imagination Chocolatier says this is one of his favorite recipes.

1⅔ cups milk
½ vanilla bean, split lengthwise
1   red chili pepper, split, seeds removed
1   cinnamon stick
1½ ounces bittersweet chocolate, grated

Pour milk into a small saucepan. Scrape in seeds from vanilla bean, then add bean. Add chili pepper and cinnamon stick. Heat to a simmer. Simmer 1 minute. Whisk in chocolate. Simmer until chocolate melts. Remove from heat. Let steep 2 minutes.

Remove vanilla bean, chili pepper and cinnamon stick. Pour into mugs and serve immediately.

MAKES 12 SERVINGS

Who says punch needs to be fruity or that melted chocolate must be served hot? Not Daniel Cooper of Pure Imagination Chocolatier, who shared this recipe.

- 2 cups hot water
- 4 ounces semisweet chocolate, chopped
- ½ cup sugar
- 2 quarts milk
- 2 teaspoons vanilla
- 1 quart vanilla ice cream (preferably Jeni's)
- 1 quart club soda

Combine hot water, chocolate and sugar in a large heavy saucepan. Bring to a boil, whisking constantly. Add milk. Heat through. Beat in vanilla with a whisk. Remove from heat. Cool. Refrigerate until well chilled.

Scoop ice cream into a punch bowl. Add chocolate mixture, then add club soda. Ladle into cups.

Fresh Pomegranate Juice Mojito

MAKES 2 SERVINGS

This nonalcoholic drink recipe from Bubbles: The Tea and Juice Company will please the under-21 crowd, but adding a jigger of light rum per serving turns the drink into a tasty cocktail.

½ large lime
6 fresh mint leaves
5 pinches of sugar
2½ cups 100% pomegranate juice
    Ice
    Soda water

Place lime, mint leaves and sugar in a pitcher or glass measuring cup. Mash with the back of a spoon to release the juice of the lime and the aroma of the mint. Stir in the pomegranate juice.

Fill 2 large glasses with ice. Pour pomegranate mixture over ice. Top with soda water and serve immediately.

MAKES 4 TO 6 SERVINGS

This recipe from Kathy Rhoads of Rhoads Farm Market is a summer-fresh version of a smoothie. It's a great way to use the freshest, ripest peaches you can find.

3 cups crushed ice
3 cups peeled, pitted and sliced peaches (about 1½ pounds)
1½ cups vanilla ice cream

Combine all ingredients in a blender and whirl until creamy smooth. Serve in chilled glasses.

Summer Thyme Mojito

This recipe is from Delayne Williams and Lynn Miller of Summer Thyme Farm. It's a great way to use the fresh mint leaves from their farm – or your backyard. If you don't have time to make the simple syrup, just use 4 teaspoons of sugar.

1 tablespoon sugar
1 tablespoon water
12 fresh mint leaves, plus additional for garnish
½ lime
    Ice
1½ ounces (3 tablespoons) light rum, such as Bacardi
7 ounces club soda
    Lime wedge

Combine sugar and water in a small saucepan. Stir over medium heat until sugar dissolves (do not boil). Remove from heat. Cool.

Place mint leaves in a tall glass. Use a long spoon, chopstick or other kitchen utensil to gently crush the mint and release its fragrance. Squeeze lime juice over mint. Add sugar syrup. Fill glass with ice.

Add rum and club soda. Stir well. Garnish with lime wedge and mint leaves.

OHIO PRODUCE AVAILABILITY

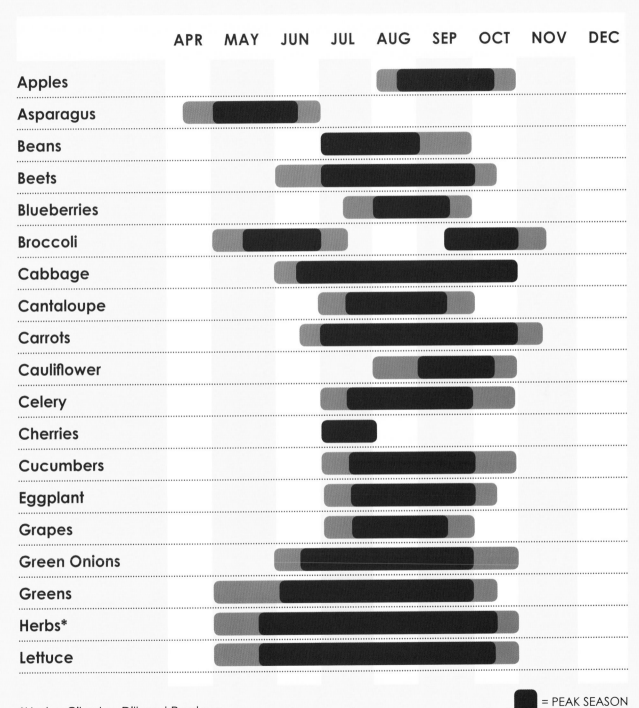

	APR	MAY	JUN	JUL	AUG	SEP	OCT	NOV	DEC
Apples									
Asparagus									
Beans									
Beets									
Blueberries									
Broccoli									
Cabbage									
Cantaloupe									
Carrots									
Cauliflower									
Celery									
Cherries									
Cucumbers									
Eggplant									
Grapes									
Green Onions									
Greens									
Herbs*									
Lettuce									

■ = PEAK SEASON

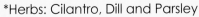

*Herbs: Cilantro, Dill and Parsley

OHIO PRODUCE AVAILABILITY

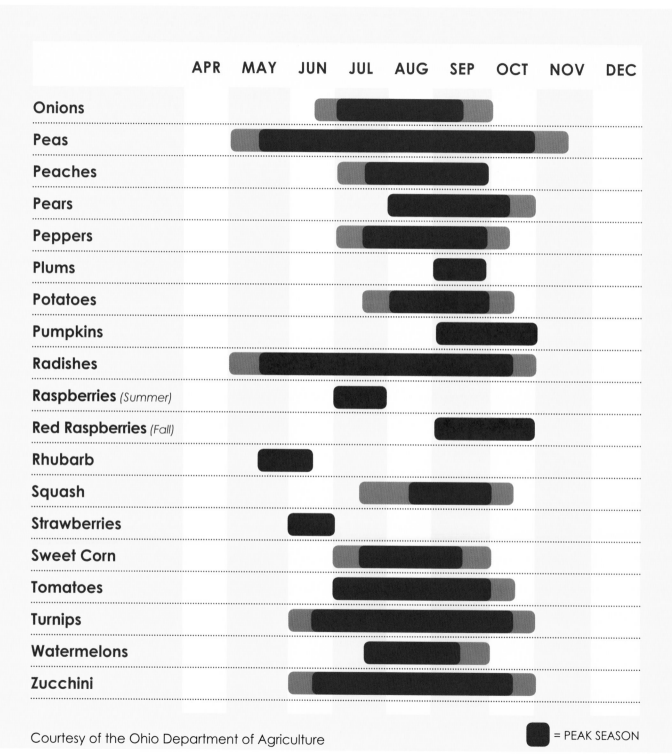

	APR	MAY	JUN	JUL	AUG	SEP	OCT	NOV	DEC

Onions

Peas

Peaches

Pears

Peppers

Plums

Potatoes

Pumpkins

Radishes

Raspberries *(Summer)*

Red Raspberries *(Fall)*

Rhubarb

Squash

Strawberries

Sweet Corn

Tomatoes

Turnips

Watermelons

Zucchini

Courtesy of the Ohio Department of Agriculture

 = PEAK SEASON

INDEX

INDEX

INDEX

INDEX